The
Garland Library
of
War and Peace

The
Garland Library
of
War and Peace

Under the General Editorship of

Blanche Wiesen Cook, *John Jay College, C.U.N.Y.*

Sandi E. Cooper, *Richmond College, C.U.N.Y.*

Charles Chatfield, *Wittenberg University*

The Crimean War: Pro and Con

comprising

Letter of John Bright, Esq., M. P., on the War

War with Russia; Its Origin and Cause
by John Alfred Langford

The War; Its Origin and Its Consequences
by Horatio Southgate

Some Observations on the War in the Crimea
by the Duke of Wellington

The Soldier that Went Not to Sebastopol
Anonymous

The Conduct of the War
by Sidney Herbert

The Close of the War
by an Income Tax Payer

with a new introduction
for the Garland Edition by
Naomi Churgin Miller

89

Garland Publishing, Inc., New York & London
1973

Library of Congress Cataloging in Publication Data
Main entry under title:

The Crimean War: pro and con.

(The Garland library of war and peace)
Reprint of Letter of John Bright, Esq., M.P., on the
war, published in 1854; of war with Russia, its origin
and cause, by J. A. Langford, published in 1855; of The
war: its origin and its consequences, by H. Southgate,
published in 1855; of Some observations on the war in
the Crimea, by the Duke of Wellington, published in 1855;
of The soldier that went not to Sebastopol, anonymous,
published in 1855; of The conduct of the war, by S.
Herbert, published in 1854; and of The close of the war,
by an income tax payer, published in 1854.
  1. Crimean War, 1853–1856--Addresses, essays,
lectures. I. Bright, John, 1811–1889. II. Series.
DK214.C74   947'.07   78-147701
ISBN 0-8240-0230-X

Printed in the United States of America

Introduction

The seven pamphlets reprinted in this volume express some of the characteristic arguments which agitated public debate in England on the origins of the Crimean War, the conduct of military operations and the kind of peace to seek at the war's end. Overwhelmingly, Englishmen justified the war on the basis of a commitment to protect the territorial integrity of Turkey and so safeguard the balance of power in Europe. The few who opposed the war denied the validity of the doctrine of balance of power, advocating instead the principle of nonintervention in the affairs of other countries as the best guide for British foreign policy. They argued that no valid British interest was at stake in the Russo-Turkish conflict and that England's decision to intervene was a tragic error. Some others defined the initial issue of Franco-Russian rivalry for control of the Holy Places and for the right to protect Christians in Turkey as a struggle between the Roman Catholic and the Orthodox Churches and warned that a Russian defeat would constitute a victory for Roman Catholicism. Represented also among these pamphlets is the view of a small group of persons, mainly Quakers, the core of the organized peace movement in Britain, who opposed this and all wars as totally incompatible with Christian teachings.

When public expectations of a swift and decisive victory over Russia were frustrated, public debate shifted to the issue of responsibility for the mismanagement of the war effort. Lord Aberdeen's government was called to an accounting and so, too, was the aristocracy, until now given pride of place in positions of political and military leadership. Disillusioned about the course of the war, the public nevertheless was prepared to support its continuance until Russia was defeated. They called for harsh terms of peace which would prohibit Russia from ever again threatening Turkey and the balance of power in Europe. Only such a peace could justify the high cost in human lives demanded by the war. Together, these pamphlets reflect the character of public opinion which became a formidable influence during the years of the Crimean War, capable of affecting decisions on the highest levels of government.

Public opinion assumed its dominant role in the years 1853-56 because support for intervention on behalf of Turkey and against Russia commanded support from all segments of the population irrespective of political loyalties or class divisions. Added to the traditional and long-held fears of Russia as a despotic power bent on territorial aggrandizement, was the memory, revived by Louis Kossuth's visit to England in 1851, of Russia's role in suppressing the revolution of 1848 in Hungary and subsequently hunting down the leaders of the rebellion. While

INTRODUCTION

Whigs and Tories spoke of Russia as a menace to the territorial integrity of Turkey and the balance of power in Europe, Radicals declaimed against her as a tyrant, suppressing the national and liberal aspirations of Poland and other minorities in Eastern Europe. War against Russia and her defeat, they believed, could usher in a new era of liberty in Europe.

Such sentiments were given expression by the press which spoke with a remarkable degree of unanimity after the news reached England of the Turkish declaration of war in October 1853 and a month later of the destruction of her fleet in the Battle of Sinope. The English public demanded intervention in order to save Turkey and spoke with such force that few newspapers could afford to stand against the tide. The Times *whose editor, John Delane, had supported the Aberdeen government and attempted to maintain an objective view, began to shift into a pro-war position in the winter of 1853. The* Edinburgh Review *and* Punch, *whose editor was a friend of the noninterventionist, Richard Cobden, deserted their former positions of neutrality and joined other newspapers in declaring Russia the enemy to be defeated. The* Manchester Guardian, *catering to an urban middle class readership and the Sunday papers read by the working classes, soon followed the lead of the* Morning Post *whose policies, dictated by Lord Palmerston, called for British intervention, and later, the resignation of Aberdeen and the accession to power of Lord Palmerston, whose strong anti-Russian*

7

views guaranteed an effective prosecution of the war. Lord Aberdeen called attention to the pressure exerted by public opinion on the government. "An English minister," he complained, "must please the newspapers, and the newspapers are always bawling for interference. They are the bullies and they make Government bully." Responding to the public clamor for war, Aberdeen felt compelled to subordinate his own wiser convictions to satisfy an irresponsible press and an impressionable public opinion.

The newspapers played an additional role in this war. For the first time newspaper readers learned directly of conditions at the front. W. H. Russell, the Times *correspondent, contrasted the stoic heroism of the soldiers with evidence of inadequate supplies, poor medical facilities, of battle plans made carelessly and military commanders who were incompetent. Shock at these revelations inflamed public opinion against the government and contributed to the demand for an investigation into the mismanagement of the war effort. When J. A. Roebuck, the Radical member for Sheffield, moved for a secret committee to inquire into the conditions of the troops before Sebastopol in January 1855 he commanded the support of the majority of members of the house of commons and also of the wider public in the country. The approval of his motion forced the resignation of Lord Aberdeen and contributed to the accession to power of Lord Palmerston. His triumph in February 1855 was also the triumph of a public opinion that*

INTRODUCTION

was determined on the energetic prosecution of the war and remained convinced of its essential righteousness.

Despite the popularity of the war, there existed a minority who had opposed it from the beginning, denying its justice and its necessity. Their views were expressed chiefly by John Bright (1811-1889), Richard Cobden (1805-1864), and the leaders of the Peace Society. Others may have agreed with their arguments but they remained silent, reluctant to stand against the powerful current of war sentiment.

Although Bright was a Quaker, and deeply influenced by Quaker principles, his opposition to the Crimean War was based on his conviction that this particular war was unnecessary and, therefore, immoral. His views on Russia and Turkey had been formulated in 1836 when visits to Constantinople, Palestine and other parts of Turkey convinced him that the country was feeble, incapable of reform and of becoming a center of trade and commerce in the Middle East. Britain as a leading commercial power had little to gain from a commitment to protect Turkish territorial integrity. On the other hand, Russia offered an expanding market for English goods, while posing no threat to Britain's naval supremacy. Moreover, as a Christian country Russian influence was far more preferable to the rule of a tottering Moslem state.

Not only did Bright call for a revision of traditional British policies towards Russia and Turkey in the

9

light of economic realities, but he, together with Richard Cobden, his partner in the agitation for the repeal of the Corn Laws, rejected the validity of the doctrine of balance of power for the conduct of British foreign policy. Believing that this doctrine was a source of wars rather than a means of avoiding disputes, Bright and Cobden advocated instead reliance on the principle of nonintervention in the affairs of other countries. Their views were reinforced by a conviction that free trade created an interdependent world in which war was an anachronism. Under such circumstances, reason dictated the discovery of peaceful methods with which to solve international problems and achieve a general disarmament. Eager to contribute their efforts to the work of like-minded men, Bright and Cobden identified themselves with the organized peace movement of their time, participating in the work of the London Peace Society and in the international peace congresses that began to meet periodically after 1843. Both men opposed the Crimean War from the start, believing that in this conflict no British interest was at stake and that from such a war no permanent and enduring gains could be secured.

Bright declared his position early in the debate and it was to remain substantially unchanged in the months ahead. In October 1853, a day after the Turkish declaration of war against Russia, refusing an invitation to attend a public meeting calling for British support to Turkey, he declared, "I cannot conceive anything more unwise than to endeavor to excite public opinion to drive the Government into war with Russia in defence of Turkey. . . . War will not save Turkey if peace cannot save her: but war will brutalize our people, increase our taxes, destroy our industry, and postpone the promised Parliamentary Reform, it may be for many years." His detailed indictment of the Government's decision to intervene appeared in his speech on the declaration of war on 31 March 1854 and in his letter to Absalom Watkin in October.

Bright focused his argument on the condition of Turkey and the role of the British government in bringing about the war. If the war was for the purpose of protecting Turkey, then Bright believed the effort was doomed to failure. Turkey was in a state of hopeless decay, threatened by insurrections at home and the increasing difficulty of maintaining her power over the Christian population of Turkish territories in Europe. Her sovereignty was an illusion, proven by the decisive influence of England on her policies and actions. But no external power could do for Turkey what she was incapable of doing for herself: reform her institutions, revitalize her economy and invigorate her administration. To fight for Turkey in the hope that she would do in the future what she failed to do in the past was foolhardy. Second, Bright placed the responsibility for the war squarely on Britain. If her ambassador, Lord Stratford de Redcliffe, had not reassured her of

11

INTRODUCTION

British support, Turkey would not have rejected Russian demands, nor the compromise spelled out in the Vienna Note of the spring of 1853 and she certainly would not have taken it upon herself to declare war on Russia. By her actions, the British government gave Turkey the power to involve Britain in war.

Moreover, the war was unjustified by reference to the doctrine of balance of power. "The whole notion was a mischievous delusion." Turkey had been excluded from the application of balance of power formerly as were other more important countries. Besides, to assume that a "balance" could emerge from a war against Russia was a delusion. No victory could make Turkey equal to Russian power in the future, nor could defeat in war effectively weaken Russia's capacity to renew her demands at a more opportune time. No British interests were involved to enhance the reasons for her intervention, but domestic reforms, desperately needed and long overdue, would be put aside again. Last, Bright dealt with the argument least capable of influencing him, the assertion that the public demand for war made it impossible to resist. "I despise," he said bitingly, "the man who says a word in favour of this war . . . because the press and a portion of the people urge the Government to enter into it."

This was basically the argument of his letter to Mr. Absalom Watkin, declining an invitation to appear at a meeting of the Manchester Patriotic Fund in

12

October 1854. He spelled out the evidence for holding Britain responsible for the war, adding his opinion, by now familiar, that the effort to uphold Turkish power was "an absurdity," and he concluded his recital of events that culminated in war with the charge that the behavior of the British government "was marked by an imbecility perhaps without example." Since this letter was reprinted in the St. Petersburg journal as well as in other European journals, Bright's critique brought upon him a fury of denunciation. Stigmatized as unpatriotic, his Manchester constituents, entertaining a motion to dissociate them from his anti-war views, made it impossible for him to speak in his own defense. He was later burned in effigy, ridiculed as

> *This broad-brimm'd hawker of holy things*
> *Whose ear is stuff'd with cotton, and rings*
> *Even in dreams to the chink of his pence.*

and in 1857 deprived of his Manchester seat in the general election.

Unlike Cobden who decided that once a shot was fired in war, rational debate was at an end and resolved that the better policy was to remain silent, Bright continued to express his unpopular point of view at public meetings and in parliament. Whereas he found himself increasingly unable to reach his audience outside Westminster, Bright evoked respect, and even emotion, in the House of Commons. One of the

13

most eloquent orators in an age which witnessed great flights of oratory, Bright commanded attention from the first expression of his dissenting opinions, to his last statement on the terms of peace. On 13 March 1854, when Bright criticized the behavior of Lord Palmerston and other ministers at a Reform Club dinner in honor of Sir Charles Napier's departure to assume his command of the Baltic fleet, Macaulay remarked, "I heard Bright say everything I thought: and I heard Palmerston and Graham expose themselves lamentably . . . I came home quite dispirited." On 22 December 1854 when Bright, ill with a severe cold, addressed the house at 1:00 A.M. on a motion to raise 15,000 foreign troops, his speech was so moving that before he got halfway through, "every man on the Ministerial Bench was in a state of acuteness such as is not witnessed in a lifetime." The government could not supply anyone to speak in rebuttal. Finally, Bright reached a climax in his own career as an orator when he spoke in the debate on the resignation of the Peelites from Palmerston's government on 22 February 1855. His peroration which began with the words: "An Angel of Death has been abroad throughout the land: you may almost hear the beating of his wings," thrilled a sceptical and sophisticated audience into silence. No matter how distasteful was Bright's criticism of the war, the House, not the public out of doors, gave him the respectful hearing he sought. His experience was additional evidence of the inadequacy of public opinion as a decisive force in the resolution of important problems of state.

Bright and Cobden were joined in their effort to speak sense to the British people on the subject of the Crimean War by the leaders and the supporters of the Peace Society. The heart of the opposition to the war was the Quakers who founded the London Peace Society in 1816, organized local branches throughout Britain, and distributed tracts and pamphlets to propagate their ideals. The Peace Society proclaimed the basic incompatibility of war with Christian teachings. All war was evil and no one who called himself a believing Christian could, in conscience, justify the taking of human life, no matter the cause. But it was not until the 1840s when the cause of peace attracted the support of public men like Cobden and Bright that the organized movement began to command attention. They called for binding arbitration of international disputes, the rejection of all war loans, the creation of an international authority and the achievement of disarmament. Such measures could end wars and make peace an enduring reality. Because of the new direction of peace efforts, support arose for their objectives. Testifying to the effectiveness of peace agitation was the outstanding role of the British delegations in the international peace congresses of the 1840s.

The Crimean War ended a promising chapter in the movement's history. As a last desperate effort to avert the war, Joseph Sturge and some of the Friends decided on a direct appeal to the Czar. They received a courteous reception in February 1854 but the Czar's response offered them no hope of any success for their mission. Yet, despite their weakness in numbers and influence during the war the pacifists were able by sheer persistence to win some recognition of their views at the Peace Congress in Paris in 1856. Through their ability to win the sympathetic support of Lord Clarendon, the British delegate to the Congress, Protocol 25 was added to the peace treaty. This called upon all states to use mediation as a method of settling their disputes with another state.

By the time the war ended, its original cause was lost in a counterpoint of war and negotiation, both paralleling each other from 1853-56. The actual conflict over the Holy Places was settled in May 1853. The Russian occupation of Moldavia and Wallachia which had provoked the Turkish declaration of war ended in June 1854 when, in response to an Austrian ultimatum, the Russians withdrew from the Danubian principalities. Peace could have come in the spring of 1855 when negotiations at Vienna seemed on the verge of success had it not been for Palmerston's desire for victories to strengthen Britain's negotiating hand at the peace table. When peace finally was concluded the terms proved so disappointing to the British public that no celebration attended the announcement.

The domestic consequences of the Crimean War proved in many ways to be more enduring than the provisions of the Peace of Paris. Roebuck's Committee of Inquiry into the management of the war was the first time that a parliamentary committee won the right to investigate the Government. The lacklustre performance of the military command, led to an attack on the aristocratic monopoly of offices in the army, and serious questioning of the range of values which had elevated the aristocracy into their positions of leadership. As a result of the Crimean War, businessmen and business virtues challenged the traditional confidence in men who were born to rule, and in amateurism in positions of leadership. Henry Layard's Administrative Reform Association, took up the agitation outside parliament for promotion based upon merit and won its objective in 1870. Because of disillusionment with the way in which the war was administered from Westminster, military administration was radically reformed. Most important, however, was the experience of the power of public opinion, expressed primarily through the newspapers but also in pamphlets and public meetings. The Crimean War, concluded Seton-Watson, "will remain beyond all question as the classical proof that in foreign policy the voice of the people is not necessarily the voice of God, and that an ill-informed and excitable public opinion can plunge a country into war no less effectually than a dictator or crowned autocrat."

Naomi C. Miller, Hunter College - C.U.N.Y.

THE LETTER

OF

JOHN BRIGHT, ESQ., MP..

ON

THE WAR,

VERIFIED AND ILLUSTRATED

BY EXTRACTS FROM THE

PARLIAMENTARY DOCUMENTS, &c.

If I had not lived long enough to be little surprised at anything, I should have been in some degree astonished at the continued rage of several gentlemen, who, not satisfied with carrying fire and sword into America, are animated nearly with the same fury against those neighbours of theirs, whose only crime it is, that they have charitably and humanely wished them to entertain more reasonable sentiments, and not always to sacrifice their interest to their passion. All this rage against unresisting dissent convinces me, that at bottom they are far from satisfied they are in the right. For what is it they would have? War? They certainly have at this moment the blessing of something that is very like one ; and if the war they enjoy at present be not sufficiently hot and extensive, they may shortly have it as warm and as spreading as their hearts can desire. Is it the force of the kingdom they call for? They have it already ; and if they choose to fight the battles in their own person, nobody prevents their setting sail to the scene of war in the next transports. . . . . . . They are continually boasting of unanimity, or calling for it. But before this unanimity can be a matter either of wish or congratulation, we ought to be pretty sure that we are engaged in a rational pursuit. Frenzy does not become a slighter distemper on account of the number of those who may be infected with it. Delusion and weakness produce not one mischief the less, because, they are universal.—(*Burke on the American War, in his Letter to the Sheriffs of Bristol.*)

LONDON:

W. & F. G. CASH, 5, BISHOPSGATE STREET WITHOUT.

Price One Penny each, or Seven Shillings per Hundred.

THE LETTER, &c.

MR. ABSALOM WATKIN, of Manchester, having invited Mr. Bright to a meeting for the Patriotic Fund about to be held in that city, and having stated that in his opinion the present war was justified by the authority of *Vattel*, Mr. Bright replied in the subjoined letter.

The letter is now published with notes, substantiating its statements by copious extracts from the *Blue Books* and other documents. In the Editor's judgment, they triumphantly verify all Mr. Bright's main positions. The despatches, however, are mutilated in such a manner, as to give reason to believe, that if they were published in a perfect state, they would make out even a more formidable case against those who have originated this war.

Rhyl, North Wales, October 29th.

MY DEAR SIR,—I think, on further consideration, you will perceive that the meeting on Thursday next would be a most improper occasion for a discussion as to the justice of the war. Just or unjust, the war is a fact, and the men whose lives are miserably thrown away in it have clearly a claim upon the country, and especially upon those who, by the expression of opinions favourable to the war, have made themselves responsible for it. I cannot, therefore, for a moment, appear to discourage the liberality of those who believe the war to be just, and whose utmost generosity, in my opinion, will make but a wretched return for the ruin they have brought upon hundreds of families.

With regard to the war itself, I am not surprised at the difference between your opinion and mine, if you decide a question of this nature, by an appeal to *Vattel*. The "law of nations" is not my law, and at best it is a code full of confusion and contradictions, having its foundation on custom, and not on a higher morality; and on custom which has always been determined by the will of the strongest. It may be a question of some interest whether the first crusade was in accordance with the law and principles of *Vattel*; but whether the first crusade was just, and whether the policy of the crusades was a wise policy, is a totally different question. I have no doubt that the American war was a just war according to the principles laid down by writers on the "law of nations," and yet no man in his senses in this country will now say that the policy of George III. towards the American colonies was a wise policy, or that war a righteous war. The French war, too, was doubtless just according to the same authorities; for there were fears, and anticipated dangers to be combatted, and law and order to be sustained in Europe; and yet few intelligent men now believe the French war to have been either necessary or just. You must excuse me if I refuse altogether to put my faith upon *Vattel*. There have been writers on international law, who have attempted to show that private assassination and the poisoning of wells were justifiable in war: and perhaps it would be difficult to demonstrate wherein these horrors differ from some of the practices which are now in vogue. I will not ask you to mould your opinion on these points by such writers, nor shall I submit my judgment to that of *Vattel.*

The question of this present war is in two parts—first, was it necessary for us to interfere by arms in a dispute between the Russians and the Turks ; and secondly, having determined to interfere, under certain circumstances, why was not the whole question terminated when Russia accepted the Vienna note ? The seat of war is 3,000 miles away from us. We had not been attacked—not even insulted in any way. Two independent Governments had a dispute, and we thrust ourselves into the quarrel. That there was some ground for the dispute is admitted by the four powers in the proposition of the Vienna note.* But

* All who have been, in any way, concerned in these negotiations on behalf of England, acknowledge this. Thus, Colonel Rose, who was *Chargé d'Affairs* at Constantinople, in Lord Stratford de Redcliffe's absence, in a despatch to Lord John Russell, dated March 7th, 1853, detailing a conversation he had just held with M. D'Ozeroff, the Russian Ambassador, represents himself to have said, " that certainly the Ottoman Minister had been to blame in the matter of the Holy Places, but that he had been coerced."—*Blue Book*, part i. p. 87.

Again,—Lord Stratford de Redcliffe writing to the Earl of Clarendon, from " Constantinople, April 9th, 1853," says :—" Your Lordship will perceive, that the Russian Ambassador does not object, by his demands, to such privileges as are known to have been obtained latterly by France, in favour of the Latins, and that his principal aim is to fix and secure the present state of possession and usage by that kind of formal and explicit agreement, which may preclude all further pretensions on the side of France, and make the Porte directly responsible to Russia for any future innovation respecting the Holy Places. *This is fair and reasonable enough in the view of an impartial observer.*"—*Blue Book*, part i. p. 127.

Again, in a despatch, dated May 22nd, 1853, he says :—" It is but justice to admit that Russia had something to complain of in the affair of the Holy Places ; nor can it be denied, that much remains to be done for the welfare and security of the Christian population in Turkey."—*Blue Book*, part i. p. 235.

Lord John Russell, in a despatch to Sir G. H. Seymour, dated "Foreign Office, February 9th, 1853" says :—" The more the Turkish Government adopts the rules of impartial law and equal administration, the less will the Emperor of Russia find it necessary to apply that exceptional protection which His Imperial Majesty has found so burthensome and inconvenient, THOUGH NO DOUBT PRESCRIBED BY DUTY, AND SANCTIONED BY TREATY." His Lordship at the same time volunteered the following character of the Emperor of Russia and his policy :—" Upon the whole, Her Majesty's Government are persuaded that NO COURSE OF POLICY CAN BE ADOPTED MORE WISE, MORE DISINTERESTED, MORE BENEFICIAL TO EUROPE, THAN THAT WHICH HIS IMPERIAL MAJESTY HAS SO LONG FOLLOWED, and which will render his name more illustrious than that of the most famous Sovereigns who have sought immortality by unprovoked conquest and ephemeral glory."—*Eastern Papers*, part v. p. 8.

The Earl of Clarendon, in a letter to Sir G. H. Seymour, dated "Foreign Office, April 5th, 1853," says :—" Viscount Stratford de Redcliffe was instructed to bear in mind, that Her Majesty's Government, without professing to give an opinion on the subject, were not insensible to the superior claims of Russia, both as respected the treaty obligations of

for the English Minister at Constantinople and the Cabinet at home the dispute would have settled itself, and the last note of Prince Menschikoff would have been accepted, and no human being can point out any material difference between that note and the Vienna note, afterwards agreed upon and recommended by the Governments of England, France, Austria and Prussia. But our Government would not allow the dispute to be settled. Lord Stratford de Redcliffe held private interviews with the Sultan—did his utmost to alarm him—insisted on his rejection of all terms of accommodation with Russia, and promised him the armed assistance of England if war should arise.*

The Turks rejected the Russian note, and the Russians crossed the Pruth, occupying the Principalities as a "material guarantee." I do not defend this act of Russia: it has always appeared to me impolitic and immoral; but I think it likely it could be well defended out of *Vattel*, and it is at least as justifiable as the conduct of Lord John Russell and Lord Palmerston in 1850, when they sent ten or twelve ships of war to the Piræus,

Turkey, and the loss of moral influence that the Emperor would sustain throughout his dominions, if, in the position occupied by His Imperial Majesty, with reference to the Greek Church, he was to yield any privileges it had hitherto enjoyed to the Latin Church, of which the Emperor of the French claimed to be the protector."—*Eastern Papers*, part v. p. 22.

To this may be added the testimony of one, who though not diplomatically engaged in the negotiations, is a competent and impartial witness, as he was on the spot during the very crisis of these transactions, viz., the Earl of Carlisle. Stating his belief that justice was on the side of the Turks, he adds:—" In giving this opinion, I do not so much allude to the actual propositions of Prince Menschikoff, for which in the outset some plausible and even some substantial grounds might be alleged; on the contrary, *I do not think it well for any Christian State to leave its co-religionists to the uncovenanted forbearance of Mussulman rulers.*"—*Diary in Turkish and Greek Waters*, p. 181.

* While the proposal of Prince Menschikoff, which had been several times modified to meet the views of the Porte, was still before it, Lord Stratford writing to the Earl of Clarendon, on May 19th, 1853, says, " on comparing notes with M. de la Cour, I found him under an impression that the Turkish Ministers were disposed to shrink from encountering the consequences of Prince Menschikoff's retirement in displeasure;" (*Blue Book*, part i. p. 177) that is, in other words, disposed to accept the note proposed by the Russian Plenipotentiary. But in a despatch written the very next day, May 10th, he describes the means he had employed to prevent their yielding to that disposition:—" In one of my preceding numbers I mentioned that I had seen the Sultan in private. The interview took place yesterday morning. Rifaat Pasha accompanied me to the Sultan's apartment, and then withdrew. Reminding the Sultan of the disposition he had shown to receive my counsels, I said that I had hitherto confided them to his Ministers, not wishing to trespass personally on His Majesty's indulgence without necessity. I added that in the present critical juncture of affairs the case might be different, and His Majesty might like to know what I thought from my own lips. " *I then endeavoured to give him a just idea of the degree of danger to which his Empire was exposed.* .... I concluded by apprising His Majesty of what I had reserved for his private ear, in order that his Ministers might take their decision without any bias from without, namely, that in the event of imminent danger I was instructed to request the Commander of Her Majesty's forces in the Mediterranean to hold his squadron in readiness."—*Blue Book*, part i. p. 213.

menacing the town with a bombardment if the dishonest pecuniary claim made by Don Pacifico were not at once satisfied.*

But the passage of the Pruth was declared by England and France and Turkey not to be a *casus belli*. Negotiations were commenced at Vienna, and the celebrated Vienna note was drawn up. This note had its origin in Paris,† was agreed to by the Conference at Vienna, ratified and approved by the Cabinets of Paris and London,‡ and pronounced by all these authorities to be such as would satisfy the honour of Russia, and at the same time be compatible with the "independence and integrity" of Turkey and the honour of the Sultan. Russia accepted this note at once,§—accepted it, I believe, by Telegraph, even before the

---

* The following is an extract from a despatch sent by Count Nesselrode to Baron Brunnow, in February, 1850, giving the Russian Government's estimation of that act of "material guarantee," on the part of England :— "It remains to be seen whether Great Britain, abusing the advantages which are afforded her by her immense maritime superiority, intends henceforth to pursue an isolated policy, without caring for those engagements which bind her to the other cabinets ; *whether she intends to disengage herself from every obligation, as well as from all community of action, and to authorize all great powers, on every fitting opportunity, to recognize towards the weak no other rule but their own will, no other right but their own physical strength.* Your Excellency will please to read this despatch to Lord Palmerston, and to give him a copy of it." But Russia did not go to war with England on account of this aggression on the rights and territories of an independent power.

† The Earl of Westmoreland writes to Lord Clarendon, under date of Vienna, July, 25th, 1853 :—"Count Buol stated that the note which had been proposed by M. Drouyn de Lhuys appeared to him to be the best foundation upon which we could proceed in the formation of the new one."—*Blue Book*, part ii. p. 19.

‡ The Earl of Clarendon writes to Lord Stratford de Redcliffe from the "Foreign Office, August 2nd, 1853. Her Majesty's Government have, in preference to all other plans, adhered to this project of note as the means best calculated to effect a speedy and satisfactory solution of the differences. They consider that it fully guards the principle for which throughout we have been contending, and *that it may therefore with perfect safety be signed by the Porte ;* and they further hope that your Excellency, before the receipt of this despatch, will have found no difficulty in procuring the assent of the Turkish Government to *a project which the Allies of the Sultan unanimously concur in recommending for his adoption.*"—*Blue Book*, part ii. p. 27.

Lord Cowley, writing to Lord Clarendon, from Paris, August 4th, 1853, says, "M. Drouyn de Lhuys has profited by the passage of Mr. Tucker, returning by the 'Caradoc,' to write to M. de la Cour, explaining why the French Government preferred the note which had been agreed to at Vienna, to that sent by Reschid Pasha from Constantinople, and instructing him *to use all his influence with the Porte to obtain its assent to the project recommended by the Four Powers.* I have had an opportunity of conversing with the Turkish Ambassador, and I was glad to find that his Excellency has written in the same sense to his government."—*Blue Book*, part ii. p. 37.

§ Sir G. H. Seymour, in a despatch to the Earl of Clarendon, dated "St. Petersburgh, August 5th, 1853," says :—"It is my agreeable duty to acquaint your Lordship, that upon waiting upon the Chancellor this morning, he stated that he had the satisfaction of informing me, that the Emperor had signified his acceptance (*acceptation pure et simple*) of the *project de*

precise words of it had been received in St. Petersburgh.* Everybody thought the question now settled; a Cabinet Minister assured me we should never hear another word about it; "the whole thing is at an end," he said, and so it appeared for a moment. But the Turk refused the note which had been drawn up by his own arbitrators, and which Russia had accepted.† And what did the Ministers say then, and what did their organ, the *Times*, say? They said it was merely a difference about words; it was a pity the Turk made any difficulty, but it would soon be

note which had been received from Vienna, and a copy of which was dispatched on the 24th ultimo, from Vienna to Constantinople. Intelligence of the Emperor's decision will be sent off to-morrow to Baron Brunnow, and has already been conveyed by telegraph to Vienna."—*Blue Book*, part ii. p. 43.

Count Neselróde conveys the acceptance, in the following language, in a despatch, dated "St. Petersburg, August 6th, 1853," and addressed to Baron Meyendorff:—"You are aware, M. le Baron, of our august master's very sincere desire to put an end, so far as depends on him, to the anxieties felt in Europe, perhaps with a certain degree of exaggeration, in regard to our present difference with Turkey. His Majesty accordingly directs you, M. le Baron, to declare to the Ministry of the Emperor Francis Joseph, and also to your colleagues of France, England, and Prussia, that for our part we accept in its present shape the last draft of note framed at Vienna."—*Blue Book*, part ii. p. 46.

* Sir J. H. Seymour, in a letter to Lord Clarendon, dated "St. Petersburgh, August 12th, 1853," reporting a conversation he had just held with Count Nesselrode, says:—"The Chancellor resumed: 'Now,' he said, 'about the delays which we are said to be desirous of interposing. The note which is intended to settle affairs reaches us on a Tuesday; on the following day our acceptance of it, without the slightest alteration, is sent off by telegraph as far as Warsaw, and from thence by a field-jäger to Vienna, where it arrives on Saturday; we subscribe, without hesitation, to the slight changes made in the note at London and Paris, and the acknowledgment of our acquiescence reaches us again on the following Tuesday—a rapidity of communication of which there has been hitherto no example.'"—*Blue Book*, part ii. p. 50.

Again, Count Nesselrode, in a note to Baron Meyendorff, dated, "St. Petersburgh, September 7th, 1853, says:—"On the mere receipt of the first draft of note agreed upon at Vienna, and even before we knew if it would be approved at London and Paris, we announced by telegraph our adhesion to it. The draft, as finally agreed upon, was sent to us at a later period, and although it had been modified in a sense which we could not mistake, nevertheless we did not on that account retract our adhesion or raise the slightest difficulty."—*Blue Book*, part ii. p. 101.

† Lord Stratford de Redcliffe writes to the Earl of Clarendon from Therapia, August 13th, 1853:—"At an early hour this morning I waited on Reshid Pasha, and communicated to him the substance of your instructions relative to the *projet de note*, already received from Vienna. I called his attention to the strong and earnest manner in which that paper was recommended to the acceptance of the Porte, not only by Her Majesty's Government, but also by the Cabinets of Austria, France, and Prussia. I reminded him of the intelligence which had arrived from St. Petersburgh the day before by telegraph, purporting that the Emperor of Russia had signified his readiness to accept the same note."—*Blue Book*, part iv. p. 69.

The next communication from Lord Stratford to the Earl of Clarendon, dated "Therapia, August 14th, 1853," is this:—"The *projet de note* transmitted from Vienna, was laid before the Council to-day by Reshid Pasha.

settled.* But it was not settled, and why not? It is said that the Russian Government put an improper construction on the

> All the Ministers were present to the number of seventeen, including the Sheik ul Islam. *The majority of the Council declared it to be their firm intention to reject the new proposal, even if amendments were introduced.*"—*Blue Book*, part ii. p. 71.

And though they were afterwards induced somewhat to modify this very peremptory proceeding, yet the adoption of such a course shows the temper which prevailed in Turkey.

* Lord Cowley writes to Lord Clarendon from "Paris, September 2nd, 1853. M. Drouyn de Lhuys stated to me yesterday, that upon the receipt of the intelligence from Constantinople, that the Porte had refused to accept the Vienna note, he had addressed a short despatch to M. de le Cour, ... to *express the disappointment with which the Emperor had learned the little attention paid by the Sultan's Ministers to the advice of His Majesty's Allies, and* to prescribe to M. de la Cour, to use all his efforts to induce the Porte to rescind its present decision."—*Blue Book*, part iv. p. 87.

On the 10th September, 1853, Lord Clarendon writes a long despatch to Lord Stratford de Redcliffe, examining the modifications proposed in the Vienna note by the Porte, and then adds :—"In conclusion, I have to observe, that these last conditions were not made in the note sent to Vienna, and which, without them, the Porte was prepared to sign as a final settlement of the question. There is, consequently, some reason to apprehend that they have since been brought forward, under the conviction that they could not be complied with ; and should this unfortunately be the case, it will verify the prediction of your Excellency made as long ago as the 16th of July, that there would soon be more to apprehend from the rashness, than from the timidity of Turkish Ministers ; and it will soon confirm the opinion lately communicated to Her Majesty's Government, and which they gather also, from the tone of your Excellency's despatches, namely,—*that the feeling of the Turkish Government is a desire for war, founded on the conviction that France and England must still per force side with Turkey, and that the war will, therefore, be a successful one for the Sultan, and obtain for him guarantees for the future, which will materially strengthen his tottering power.*"—*Blue Book*, part iv. p. 95.

The *Times*, of September 17th, 1853, says :—"The obligations of the crisis are manifestly reciprocal. If Europe has its duties towards Turkey, Turkey has its duties towards Europe. If Europe owes protection to the Ottoman empire, that empire owes consideration to the peace of Europe. Either the Turks are competent to maintain their own rights or they are not. If they are, the whole of this discussion is eminently gratuitous, and Admiral Dundas may as well bring the fleet home from Besika Bay. If they are not, they must rely on the succour of others, and it is as clear as reason can make it that this succour must be accepted, not on their own terms, but on the terms of those who lend it. The Porte cannot pretend to combine the advantages of independence and protection. If it goes to war on its own decision and its own responsibility, it may commence hostilities at discretion ; but, if it goes to war with British ships and French soldiers, it can have no right to wrest the initiative from the hands of England and France. The four Powers have publicly acknowledged their desire and their obligation to protect the independence of Turkey, but it is perfectly preposterous to demand that when the object can be attained by pacific negotiations they should select, in preference, the process of a war, which would infallibly be terrible for humanity, and might possibly be ruinous to themselves. Such a policy would be destructive even to the very empire under protection. *What would be the results of a general war no living being could venture to conjecture ; but, if there is any one point certain, it is this*—THAT AT ITS CLOSE THERE WOULD BE NO TURKEY IN EUROPE."

Vienna note. But it is unfortunate for those who say this, that the Turk placed precisely the same construction upon it; and further it is upon record that the French Government advised the Russian Government to accept it, on the ground that "its general sense differed in nothing from the sense of the proposition of Prince Menschikoff."* It is, however, easy to see why the Russian Government should, when the Turks refused the award of their own arbitrators, re-state its original claim, that it might not be damaged by whatever concession it had made in accepting the award; and this is evidently the explanation of the document issued by Count Nesselrode, and about which so much has been said. But, after this, the Emperor of Russia spoke to Lord Westmoreland on the subject at Olmutz, and expressed his readiness to accept the Vienna note, with any clause which the Conference might add to it, explaining and restricting its meaning; † and he urged that this should be done at once, as he

* The Vienna note was avowedly founded upon, and was indeed substantially the same as the French note, previously submitted to Russia, and which had been approved by the British Government; for the Earl of Clarendon writing to the Earl of Westmoreland, July 25th, 1853, in reference to the proposal of Count Buol to frame the Vienna note, says :—"We approve of the mode of proceeding, but can give no positive sanction until we know in what manner it differs from *the French note to which we have already agreed.*"—*Blue Book*, part ii. p. 1.

Now M. Drouyn de Lhuys, who was the original framer of the note, ought surely to be assumed to know in what sense it was intended to be understood. Well, this Minister in writing to St. Petersburgh to urge the acceptance of his note, says :—"That which the cabinet of St. Petersburgh ought to desire is an act of the Porte, which testifies that it has taken into serious consideration the mission of Prince Menschikoff, and that it *renders homage* to the sympathies which an identity of religion inspires in the Emperor Nicholas for all Christians of the Eastern rite." And further on:—" *They,* (the French Government) *submit it to the Cabinet of St. Petersburgh, with the hope that it will find that its* GENERAL SENSE DIFFERS IN NOTHING FROM THE SENSE OF THE PROPOSITION PRESENTED BY PRINCE MENSCHIKOFF, *and that it gives it satisfaction on all the essential points of its demands. The slight variation in the form of it will not be observed by the masses of the people, either in Russia or in Turkey. To their eyes the step taken by the Porte will preserve all the signification which the Cabinet of St. Petersburgh wishes to give to it ; and his Majesty the Emperor Nicholas will appear to them always as the powerful and respected protector of their religious faith.*"—Cited in Count Nesselrode's Memorandum of March 2nd, 1854, as published in the *Journal des Debats.*

It is impossible that anything can be more explicit than this. How can the English and French Governments pretend that Russia interpreted the note in a sense different from what they intended, when it is expressly stated that it was presented "in the *hope* that its general sense differed in nothing from the proposition of Prince Menschikoff," and that it was designed to preserve in the eyes of the people, " *all the signification which the Cabinet of St. Petersburgh wishes to give to it ?*"

† Lord Westmoreland, writing from Olmutz, September 28th, 1853, to Lord Clarendon, says :—" That His Majesty (the Emperor of Russia) had authorized Count Nesselrode to confer with Count Buol *as to the adoption of* ANY PROPOSAL *by which a still further guarantee might be offered to the Porte,* that he would maintain inviolate the assurances he had given ; that he sought no new right, no further extension of power ; and that he

was anxious that his troops should re-cross the Pruth before

looked to nothing but the maintenance of treaties and the *status quo* in religious matters. His Majesty had directed Count Nesselrode to report for his approval, any recommendation which, in furtherance of his object, he might, in conjunction with Count Buol, consider it advisable to adopt."

And further on in the same despatch, Lord Westmoreland says :—" His Majesty the Emperor Nicholas, previous to his departure from Olmutz, which took place this evening, was pleased, on taking leave of me, *to refer to the decision he had taken with reference to this measure,* and to assure me that he had thus endeavoured, by allowing his former declarations to be strengthened by repetition, to give an additional proof of his desire to meet every legitimate wish which was expressed to him by those Powers."

The following note " explaining and restricting " the meaning of the Vienna note was accordingly adopted :—

" In recommending unanimously to the Porte to adopt the draft of note drawn up at Vienna, the Courts of Austria, France, England and Prussia are convinced that that document by no means prejudices the sovereign rights and dignity of His Majesty the Sultan.

" That conviction is founded on the positive assurances which the Cabinet of St. Petersburgh has given in regard to the intentions by which His Majesty the Emperor of Russia is animated in requiring a general guarantee of the religious immunities granted by the Sultans to the Greek Church within their empire.

" It results from these assurances that in requiring, in virtue of the principles laid down in the treaty of Kainardji, that the Greek religion and clergy should continue to enjoy their spiritual privileges under the protection of their sovereign the Sultan, the Emperor demands nothing contrary to the independence and the rights of the Sultan, nothing which implies an intention to interfere in the internal affairs of the Ottoman empire.

" What the Emperor of Russia desires, is the strict maintenance of the religious *status quo* of his religion, that is to say, an entire equality of rights and immunities between the Greek church and the other Christian communities, subjects of the Porte ; consequently, the enjoyment by the Greek church of the advantages already granted to those communities. He has no intention of resuscitating the privileges of the Greek church which have fallen into disuse by the effect of time or administrative changes, but he requires that the Sultan should allow it to share in all the advantages which he shall hereafter grant to other Christian rites."—*Blue Book,* part ii. p. 129.

Lord Westmoreland, in transmitting this proposal to the English Government, adds, " It is not believed that it ought to. be considered in any way a condition onerous to the Porte, or unfitting for it to grant." Now, let it be distinctly remarked, that not only Austria and Prussia, but France approved this proposal, and it was rejected at the instance of our Government alone. Lord Cowley, writing from Paris, October 4th, 1853, says to the Earl of Clarendon, " I saw M. Drouyn de Lhuys later in the day. . . . He then said that the Emperor was inclined to view the proposed declaration favourably ; that His Majesty thought that it guarded the points on which the French and English Governments had the most insisted."— *Blue Book,* part ii. p. 131.

Again, Lord Clarendon writes on October 7th, 1853, to Lord Cowley, to this effect :—" On the 4th instant, Count Walewski informed me *that the assurances as to the intentions of Russia contained in Count Buol's project of note, appeared satisfactory to the French Government, who were prepared with the concurrence of Her Majesty's Government, to agree to the signature of that note by the Four Representatives in Constantinople,* that it should be offered to the Porte in exchange for the note originally sent from Vienna." —*Blue Book,* part ii. p. 140.

But our Government peremptorily rejected the proposal "Lord

winter.* It was in this very week that the Turks summoned a grand council, and, contrary to the advice of England and France, determined on a declaration of war.†

Now, observe the course taken by our Government. They agreed to the Vienna note ; not fewer than five members of this Cabinet have filled the office of Foreign secretary, and therefore may be supposed capable of comprehending its meaning : it was a note drawn up by the friends of Turkey, and by arbitrators self-constituted on behalf of Turkey ; they urged its acceptance on the Russian Government, and the Russian Government accepted it ; there was then a dispute about its precise meaning, and Russia agreed, and even proposed that the arbitrators at Vienna should amend it, by explaining it, and limiting its meaning, so that no question of its intention should henceforth exist. But, the Turks having rejected it, our Government turned round, and declared the Vienna note, their own note, entirely inadmissible, and defended the conduct of the Turks in having rejected it. The Turks declared war, against the advice of the English and French Governments‡—so, at least, it appears

Clarendon writes to Lord A. Loftus, requesting him to state to Baron Manteuffel, " that it is quite impossible for Her Majesty's Government now, under any circumstances or conditions whatever, to recommend the adoption of the Vienna note to the Porte."—*Blue Book*, part ii. p. 132.

* This allusion to the withdrawal of the troops before winter seems to have had reference to the Vienna, and not the Olmutz note, for we find the Earl of Westmoreland, writing from Vienna, September 14th, 1853, says :—" Count Buol stated that Baron Mayendorff had received a second despatch from Count Nesselrode, expressing the great disappointment felt by the Emperor of Russia at the modification of the original note by the Porte, *and his regret at the consequent delay in the execution of the order which had already been prepared for commencing the evacuation of the Principalities*, and which would have taken place immediately upon the Emperor's receiving the assurance that that note had been adopted by the Porte and would be presented to him. Count Nesselrode declares in this despatch that this measure will be still carried out, if the Emperor should receive a satisfactory assurance from the Sultan *in time for the evacuation to take place during the month of October ; later in the year it would not be possible to move the troops.*"—*Blue Book*, part ii. p. 106.

† Lord Stratford de Redcliffe writes under date of Constantinople, September 26th, 1853 :—" The Turkish Council has given its decision in favour of war . . . . . The efforts of the Four Representatives to obtain a pacific solution were fruitless, as well as those which I made this morning, subsequently to the arrival in the course of the night of your despatches forwarded by the *Triton.*"—*Blue Book*, part ii. p. 130.

Again,—M. Drouyn de Lhuys, in a despatch to Count Walewski, dated Paris, October 4th, 1853, writes :—" Whilst the Russian army is approaching the Danube, the Porte, *notwithstanding the unanimous efforts of the Representatives of France, of Austria, of Great Britain, and of Prussia, and without being yet acquainted with the new interpretation which Count Nesselrode has given to the note put forth by the Conference*, has persisted for the second time, in its resolution, and declared, that this note, in its original terms, was for ever inadmissible. The Divan has unanimously devolved on the Sultan the duty of declaring war."—*Blue Book*, part ii. p. 136.

‡ They *insisted* upon war, not only against the advice, but against the almost agonising entreaties, of the Western Powers, and especially of the

from the blue-books ; but the moment war was declared by

English Government. Nothing is more manifest from the latter parts of these Blue Books, than that the Turks felt that they were absolute masters of the situation—that they could safely spurn all efforts at conciliation, because England and France had placed themselves in such a position, that according to the language of Lord Clarendon, "they must perforce side with Turkey." Thus Lord Stratford, on the 20th of September, represents himself as "*imploring*" Reshid Pacha, at least to suspend, (*Blue Book*, part ii. page 149,) the declaration of war for a short time ; and on the 1st of October, this same Reshid Pacha, after declaring that the Turkish Government had, in spite of the "imploring" entreaty of our Ambassador, "determined upon going to war," instructs the Turkish Ambassador, in London in these cool words :—"*The Imperial Government, under existing circumstances, reckons upon the moral and material support of England and France ; and it is to that object that the language which you have to hold at London should be directed.*"—(*Blue Book*, part ii. page 151.) It is clear, also, that Lord Clarendon and Lord Stratford de Redcliffe felt that they had placed England helplessly in the power of the Turks, and it would be almost ludicrous, but for the painful consequences involved, to see the eager and impotent efforts made by them both, when it was too late, to lay the spirit they had raised at Constantinople.

Lord Clarendon, writing October 24th, 1853, says :—"It is my duty to inform your Excellency, that Her Majesty's Government observe with regret that due attention has not been paid by the Turkish Government to the advice tendered by your Excellency, with a sincere regard for the Sultan's own interests, and when, with no other motive than that of preserving peace without detriment to the honour and independence of the Sultan, you desired that the declaration of war and the commencement of hostilities, should be delayed, until all attempts at negotiation should have proved unsuccessful." And what is the explanation ? Why, that the French and English had gone too far, and could not retreat, for Lord Cowley in trying to persuade M. Drouyn de Lhuys, that the Olmutz note, which the French Emperor was willing to accept, ought to be rejected, says very significantly, "I asked M. Drouyn de Lhuys whether the Emperor had considered . . . . *the position in which the two governments would find themselves, if, with their fleets before Constantinople*, they pressed the acceptance of the Vienna note, (*i.e.* with the Olmutz addition) upon the Porte, and the Porte persisted in her refusal, and war was the consequence ?"—(*Blue Book*, part ii. p. 131.) So again, Lord Stratford, writing on November 17th, 1853, after telling Lord Clarendon, that "a new proposition" presented by himself and the French Ambassador to the Porte, had no chance of acceptance, "even in a modified shape," adds :—"I have hitherto exerted my almost solitary efforts in favour of peace under every conceivable disadvantage, including *even that which results in Turkish estimation, from the presence of the allied squadrons in these waters.*"—(*Blue Book*, part ii. p. 271.) Writing later on the same day, he says :—"Your Lordship may be assured that I omitted nothing which my instructions, my recollections, or my reflection could suggest, in order to make an impression on his (Reshid Pacha's) mind. *I lament to say that all my efforts were unavailing.* . . . I did, however, the only thing which remained for me to do at the moment. *I took my leave with evident marks of disappointment and dissatisfaction, expressing in strong terms my apprehension, that the Pacha would one day have reason to look back with painful regret on the issue of our interview.*"—(*Blue Book*, part ii. p. 281.)

Lord Stratford next tries the Sultan himself, in presenting to him "Vice Admiral Dundas and the officers under his command." The result he describes in the following language : "After the officers had retired, I saw the Sultan in private, and availed myself of the opportunity . . . . to press the arguments I had already employed in favour of peace. What-

Turkey, our Government openly applauded it. England, then, was committed to the war. She had promised armed assistance to Turkey—a country without government,* and whose adminis-

ever impression I may have made on his Majesty's mind—and his manner encouraged some hope in that respect, especially on the score of humanity, and of the approach of winter—*his language was in complete accordance with that of his minister.*"—(*Blue Book*, part ii. p. 288.) And when at length the importunities and reproaches of the Western Powers extorted from the Porte a reluctant promise to suspend the commencement of hostilities, for a few days, that promise was broken. Lord Clarendon writing to Lord Stratford, November 8th, 1853, says:—" Her Majesty's Government entirely approve the proceedings adopted by your Excellency, as reported in your despatch of the 21st ultimo, for preventing the commencement of hostilities, and *they much regret that the promise you obtained to that effect should not have been acted upon.* Her Majesty's Government are anxious to receive the explanation upon this subject, which your Excellency has doubtless demanded from the Porte."—(*Blue Book*, part ii. p. 219.)

* Lord Clarendon, in his letter of instructions to Lord Stratford, when returning to Constantinople, says:—" *The accumulated grievances of foreign nations, which the Porte is unable or unwilling to redress, the mal-administration of its own affairs, and the increasing weakness of the executive power in Turkey,* have caused the allies of the Porte latterly to assume a tone alike novel and alarming, and which, if persevered in, may lead to a general revolt among the Christian subjects of the Porte, and prove fatal to the independence and integrity of the empire. . . .

" Your Excellency's long residence at the Porte, and intimate knowledge of the affairs of Turkey, will enable you to point out those reforms and improvements which the Sultan, under his present difficulties, may have the means of carrying into effect, and in what manner the Porte may best establish a system of administration calculated to afford reasonable security for the development of its commercial measures and the maintenance of its independence, *recognised by the great Christian Powers on presumption of its proving a reality,* and a stable bond of peace in their respective relations with the Porte, and generally through the Levant. *Nor will you disguise from the Sultan and his Ministers that perseverance in their present course must end in alienating the sympathies of the British nation, and making it impossible for Her Majesty's Government to shelter them from the impending danger, or to overlook the exigencies of Christendom exposed to the natural consequences of their unwise policy and reckless mal-administration.*"—*Blue Book*, part i. pp. 81, 82.

Lord Stratford writing to M. E. Pisani, from Therapia, June 22nd 1853, says:—" You will communicate to Reschid Pacha the several extracts of consular reports from Scutari, Monastir, and Prevesa, annexed to this instruction. You will observe that *they relate in part to those acts of disorder, injustice, and corruption, sometimes of a very atrocious kind, which I have frequently brought by your means to the knowledge of the Ottoman Porte.* It is with extreme disappointment and pain, that I observe the continuance of evils which affect so deeply the welfare of the empire, and which assume a deeper character of importance in the present critical state of the Porte's relations with Russia."—*Blue Book*, part i. p. 383.

Again,—in July 4th, he writes :—" *I have frequently had occasion of late and indeed for some years back, to bring to the knowledge of the Porte, such atrocious instances of cruelty, rapine, and murder, as I have found, with extreme concern, in the Consular reports, exhibiting generally the disturbed and misgoverned condition of Roumelia, and calling loudly for redress from the Imperial Government. The character of these disorderly and brutal outrages may be said with truth, to be in general, that of Mussulman fanati-*

tration was at the mercy of contending factions ; and incapable of fixing a policy for herself, she allowed herself to be dragged on by the current of events at Constantinople. She " drifted," as Lord Clarendon said, exactly describing his own position, into the war, apparently without rudder and without compass.

The whole policy of our Government in this matter is marked with an imbecility perhaps without example. I will not say they intended a war from the first, though there are not wanting many evidences that war was the object of at least a section of the Cabinet. A distinguished member of the House of Commons said to a friend of mine, immediately after the accession of the present Government to office, " You have a war Ministry, and you will have a war." But I leave this question to point out the disgraceful feebleness of the Cabinet, if I am to absolve them from the guilt of having sought occasion for war. They promised the Turk armed assistance on conditions, or without conditions. They, in concert with France, Austria, and Prussia, took the original dispute out of the hands of Russia and Turkey, and formed themselves into a court of arbitration in the interests of Turkey ; they made an award, which they declared to be safe and honourable for both parties ; this award was accepted by Russia and rejected by Turkey ; and they then turned round upon their own award, declared it to be " totally inadmissible," and made war upon the very country whose Government, at their suggestion and urgent recommendation, had frankly accepted it. At this moment England is engaged in a murderous warfare with Russia, although the Russian Government accepted her own terms of peace, and has been willing to accept them in the sense of England's own interpretation of them ever since they were offered ; and at the same time England is allied with Turkey, whose Government rejected the award of England, and who entered into the war in opposition to the advice of England. Surely, when the Vienna note was accepted by Russia, the Turks should have been prevented from going to war, or should have been allowed to go to war at their own risk.

I have said nothing here of the fact that all these troubles have sprung out of the demands made by France upon the Turkish Government, and urged in language more insulting than any which has been shown to have been used by Prince

<hr/>

cism, excited by cupidity and hatred against the Sultan's Christian subjects. . . . . The more pressing and obvious wants are these ; the correction, by means of explanation and control, of that fanatical and licentious spirit which now influences the Mussulman population ; some special means for the protection of the loyal and peaceably disposed, whether Mussulman or Rayah, an efficient responsibility on the part of the local governors and magistrates towards the Supreme Government ; a more regular and judicious exercise of authority in the collection of supplies, and the direction of persons acting in concert with the army ; relief for the labouring and rural classes. &c."—*Blue Book*, part i. pp. 383–4. That is, in other words, " the pressing and obvious wants," included almost everything necessary to constitute an organized government.

Menschikoff.* I have said nothing of the diplomatic war which has been raging for many years past in Constantinople, and in which England has been behind no other Power in attempting to subject the Porte to foreign influences.† I have said nothing

* Col. Rose, writing to the Earl of Malmesbury, November 20th, 1852, says :—" M. de Lavelette, (the French Ambassador at Constantinople,) has induced the Porte to address him a note, which nullifies the *status quo* established by the Firman to the Greeks, and states that nothing can be done by the Porte affecting the treaty of 1740, without the consent of France. The French Government have expressed their approbation of this note." He is represented as "announcing the extreme measures he would take should the Porte leave any engagements to him unfulfilled." "He has," it is added, "more than once, talked of the appearance, in that case, of a French fleet off Jaffa; and once he alluded to a French occupation of Jerusalem, when, he said, we shall have all the sanctuaries !" (*Blue Book*, part i. p. 49.)

Lord John Russell, in a despatch to Lord Cowley, dated Foreign Office, January 28, 1853, says :—" But her Majesty's Government cannot avoid perceiving that the Ambassador of France at Constantinople was the first to distrust the *status quo* in which the matter rested, and if report is to be believed, the French Ambassador was the first to speak of having recourse to force, and to threaten the intervention of a French fleet, to enforce the demands of his country."—(*Blue Book*, part i. p. 67.)

† Many illustrations of this might be given, but we restrict ourselves to one, which seems to be an almost exact counterpart of that for which Russia is now so vehemently condemned. In 1841, our own government united with the King of Prussia, in making certain demands of the Porte on behalf of the Protestants in Turkey. Lord Palmerston on July 26th, 1841, thus wrote to Lord Ponsonby, then our Ambassador at Constantinople:—"I have to acquaint your Excellency, that the government of Her Majesty adopts with great earnestness the plan proposed by the King of Prussia, as detailed in the enclosed paper, for affording to European Protestants encouragement to settle and purchase land in the Turkish dominions, and for securing to Protestants, *whether native subjects of the Porte* or foreigners who have settled in Turkey, securities, and protection *similar to those which Christians of other denominations enjoy,*"—(the very same thing that the Czar asked for the Greeks). The first instalment of this demand was for permission to build a protestant church at Jerusalem. This was refused by the Ottoman Court. Lord Ponsonby writes to Lord Aberdeen thus :—"I had a final interview with Rifat Pasha this day, at which I renewed all the arguments in support of the demand for permission to build a church at Jerusalem. The Pasha will send me an official note on the 9th, containing his reply to what I have said on the subject, and *containing the refusal of the demand.* The Ottoman ministers are not personally averse to what has been asked, but they are overruled by the fears of the Ulemas in the council, having Sheik Al Islam at their head. I spoke strongly to Rifaat and pointed out the risk the Porte incurred of giving offence to Her Majesty's Government, *by denying to them that which they had granted to others*, and told him that he was in error when he denied our right; and I claimed it, not only on the ground set forth in my official note, but specifically on the right of the most ancient of our customs. I maintained that we have a right, founded on treaty, *that all the privileges, of every kind, granted to the French, should be considered as belonging equally to us,* and that to refuse them would possibly be considered an insult. His Excellency Rifaat Pasha said it was no insult. I replied, that, *unfortunately, it did not depend on the opinion of His Excellency, and that Her Majesty's Government might think it an insult.*" In a letter afterwards addressed by Lord Ponsonby to Rifaat Pasha, he clenches the matter with the following very significant threat :—" IT REMAINS FOR YOUR EXCELLENCY TO CONSIDER WHAT MAY BE THE CONSEQUENCES OF A VIOLATION BY THE SUBLIME PORTE

of the abundant evidences there is that we are not only at war with Russia, but with all the Christian population of the Turkish empire, and that we are building up our Eastern Policy on a false foundation—namely, on the perpetual maintenance of the most immoral and filthy of all despotisms over one of the fairest portions of the earth which it has desolated, and over a population it has degraded but has not been able to destroy. I have said nothing of the wretched delusion that we are fighting for civilization in supporting the Turk against the Russian and against the subject Christian population of Turkey. I have said nothing about our pretended sacrifices for freedom in this war, in which one great and now dominant ally is a monarch who, last in Europe, struck down a free constitution, and dispersed by military violence a national Representative Assembly.

My doctrine would have been non-intervention in this case. The danger of the Russian power was a phantom ;* the necessity of permanently upholding the Mahometan rule in Europe is an absurdity. Our love for civilization, when we subject the Greeks and Christians to the Turks, is a sham; and our sacrifices for freedom, when working out the behests of the Emperor of the French and coaxing Austria to help us, is a pitiful imposture. The evils of non-intervention were remote and vague, and could neither be weighed nor described in any accurate terms. The good we can judge something of already, by estimating the cost of a contrary policy. And what is that cost? War in the north and south of Europe, threatening to involve every country of Europe. Many, perhaps fifty millions sterling, in the course of expenditure by this country alone, to be raised from the taxes of a people whose extrication from ignorance and poverty can only be hoped for from the continuance of peace. The disturbance of trade throughout the world, the derangement of monetary affairs, and difficulties and ruin to thousands of families. Another year of high prices of food, notwithstanding a full harvest in England, chiefly because war interferes with imports, and we have declared our principal foreign food-growers to be our enemies.† The loss of human life to an enormous extent.

OF ITS TREATIES WITH GREAT BRITAIN."—*Blue Book*, Correspondence respecting the Condition of Protestants in Turkey, 1841-51, pp. 5-8. The Porte yielded, of course ; but if it had not, does any man doubt that England would have made some naval demonstration by way of "material guarantee" for the accomplishment of her wish?

* "There never has been a great state whose power for external aggression has been more overrated than Russia. She may be impregnable within her own boundaries, BUT SHE IS NEARLY POWERLESS FOR ANY PURPOSE OF OFFENCE."—*Lord Palmerston, in the House of Commons last session.*

† "*The people—the many-handed, many-mouthed people—will apparently have to pay this same year 30s. a quarter, or 37 per cent. more for their bread than they did last year.* Perhaps the most striking way of putting it, is to remind the working classes that every man, woman, and child is supposed to consume, one with another, a quarter of wheat a-year ; so that the head of a family of five persons will find that his year's bread will cost £7 10s. more than last year. . . . . There is no deficiency which the Black Sea could not easily supply. But there is the difficulty. Wheat

Many thousands of our own countrymen have already perished of pestilence and in the field; and hundreds, perhaps thousands, of English families will be plunged into sorrow, as a part of the penalty to be paid for the folly of the nation and its rulers.

When the time comes for the "inquisition for blood," who shall answer for these things? You have read the tidings from the Crimea; you have, perhaps, shuddered at the slaughter; you remember the terrific picture,—I speak not of the battle, and the charge, and the tumultuous excitement of the conflict, but of the field after the battle—Russians in their frenzy or their terror, shooting Englishmen who would have offered them water to quench their agony of thirst; Englishmen, in crowds, rifling the pockets of the men they had slain or wounded, taking their few shillings or roubles, and discovering among the plunder of the stiffening corpses images of the "Virgin and the Child." You have read this, and your imagination has followed the fearful details. This is war,—every crime which human nature can commit or imagine, every horror it can perpetrate or suffer; and this it is which our Christian Government recklessly plunges into, and which so many of our countrymen at this moment think it patriotic to applaud! You must excuse me if I cannot go with you. I will have no part in this terrible crime. My hands shall be unstained with the blood which is being shed. The necessity of maintaining themselves in office may influence an administration; delusions may mislead a people; *Vattel* may afford you a law and a defence; but no respect for men who form a Government, no regard I have for "going with the stream," and no fear of being deemed wanting in patriotism, shall influence me in favour of a policy which, in my conscience, I believe to be as criminal before God as it is destructive of the true interest of my country.

I have only to ask you to forgive me for writing so long a letter. You have forced it from me, and I would not have written it did I not so much appreciate your sincerity and your good intentions towards me.

Believe me to be, very sincerely yours, .
JOHN BRIGHT.

Absalom Watkin, Esq., Manchester.

that would fetch 70s. or 80s. here, is only worth 20s. in ports affected by our blockade. The operations of war are of first necessity; and, hard as it may seem to deprive the poor corn-grower of his price, unreasonable as it may seem to deprive the British workman of cheap bread, still, if the blockade is necessary for the reduction of the foe, there is no help for it."— *Times.*

RICHARD BARRETT, Printer, 13, Mark Lane, London.

THE

WAR WITH RUSSIA;

Its Origin and Cause:

A REPLY TO THE LETTER OF J. BRIGHT, ESQ., M.P.

BY

JOHN ALFRED LANGFORD.

LONDON:

R. THEOBALD, PATERNOSTER ROW.

1855.

BIRMINGHAM:
PRINTED BY J. A. LANGFORD, ANN-STREET.

THE WAR WITH RUSSIA.

AMID the din of arms and the fierce contest of battle, the less harmful, but, perhaps, not the less potent war of opinion, the clash of controversy, the dissemination of "views," are as busy at their work as in the piping times of peace. As might have been anticipated, the terrible struggle in which we are engaged has absorbed every other feeling: and whether men agree or disagree respecting the cause, the necessity, and the justness of the war, all are zealous and earnest in advocacy or opposition. A vast majority of the nation believe in the justness of England's position —believe that she exhausted every means, and even went beyond the strict line of national respect, in seeking to stay the hand of him who, in sanctimonious phrase, was ever ringing changes on the theme of peace, and yet proved himself so eager to "cry havoc, and let slip the dogs of war"—believe that no other course was open to her—believe that if she wished to preserve her own dearly-won liberties, she must stoutly oppose any further encroachments on the rights and liberties of Turkey. A vast majority of the nation were, and still are, firmly convinced of this, and have most emphatically declared the firmness of that conviction by the enthusiasm of their support and the wonderful liberality of their purses. Yet, notwithstanding the clearness with which our course was marked out for us—notwithstanding the steady and continuous aggression of Russia, now by secret fraud and now by open force, since the time of Peter I. to the present day—there is a party in England, and there are a number of Englishmen, who, taking pre-conceived views to their study of the question, profess to find in the Blue Books—in the documents issued by the Governments of the great nations, England, France, Turkey, and Russia —sufficient reason to condemn the policy which England has adopted, and to declare the war dishonourable, unjust, and disgraceful. Among the party taking this view are men of wealth and influence, and no pains or expense is spared in propagating their opinions. Lecturers are busy going from town to town disseminating partial and *ex parte* statements of the cause of the war; and letters and speeches, to which are added carefully collected extracts from the Blue Books, are printed and gratuitously distributed by thousands in order to indoctrinate the people with falsely-called peace principles. The purpose of the present tract is to examine the pretensions of this party, to test its statements, to complete the quotations which have been so partially made, and by presenting a *full* statement of facts, to enable the people to judge for themselves of the worth of that advocacy and the justice of that cause which has to resort to such expedients for its support and defence.

Mr. BRIGHT, in his Letter to Mr. ABSALOM WATKIN, says that "we are not only at war with Russia, but with all the Christian population of the Turkish Empire;" and Mr. GEORGE THOMPSON, in his Lecture on the War, corroborated this statement by the curiously bold assertion, that the "Greek Christians, who formed the mass of the population of Turkey in Europe, were of a common faith, common hope, and acknowledge a common headship with those of Russia." Now, what are the facts? The Greek Church in Turkey considers the Russian Greek Church as schismatical and heretical, and refuse, and have ever refused, to acknowledge the Patriarchship of the Emperor of Russia. Of the 11,000,000 members of the Greek Church who are the subjects of the Sultan, there are in the Principalities of Moldavia and Wallachia about 4,000,000; these, with the exception of some 50,000 Hungarian Catholics, are of the Greek, but not of the Russo-Greek, Church. Servia has also 1,000,000 of the same persuasion, and equally averse to the Russian Czar-Patriarch; Servia has also for a long time past been striving to shake off the influence of Russia, and to unite herself more closely with her rightful ruler, the Sultan. Besides these, there are 2,400,000 Eutychian Armenians, of which 40,000 belong to the Latin Church, and also more than 1,000,000 are Roman Catholics and United Greeks. *None of these recognise the Patriarchship of the Emperor of Russia.*

In order that the feeling of the Greek Church in Turkey respecting this matter may be fully understood, I quote the following passage from an address delivered by the Archimandrate Suagoaud to the Roumains, (Moldo-Wallachians) in Paris, so late as January, 1853. The occasion was this: the Roumains had asked permission from the French Government to build a chapel in Paris, and the application was received with the very pertinent question, (supposing them to be of the same Church as the Peace Society do,) "Why do you not worship in the Russian Chapel already erected in Paris?" Here is the answer: "When we expressed a desire to found a Chapel of our own rite, we were told that a Russian Chapel already existed in Paris, and we were asked why the Roumains do not frequent it. What! Roumains to frequent a Russian place of worship! Is it then forgotten that they can never enter its walls, and that the Wallachians who die in Paris, forbid, at their very last hour, that their bodies should be borne to a Muscovite Chapel, and declare that the presence of a Russian priest would be an insult to their tomb. Whence comes this irreconcilable hatred? That hatred is perpetuated by the difference of language. The Russian tongue is Sclavonic; ours is Latin. Is there, in fact, a single Roumain who understands the language of the Muscovite? That hatred is just; for is not Russia our mortal enemy? Has she not closed up our schools and debarred us from all instruction, in order to sink our people into the depths of barbarism, and to reduce them the more easily to servitude? On that hatred I pronounce a blessing; for the Russian Church is a schism the Roumains reject; because the Russian Church has separated from the great Eastern Church; because the Russian Church does not recognise as its head the Patriarch of Constantinople; because it does not receive the Holy Unction of Byzantium; because it has constituted itself into a Synod of which the Czar is the despot; and because that Synod, in obedience to his orders, has changed its worship, has fabricated an unction which it terms holy, has suppressed or changed the fast days and the Lents as established by our bishops; because it has canonised Sclavonians who are apocryphal saints, such as Vladimir, Olgo, and so many others whose names are unknown to us; because the rite of Confession, which was instituted to ameliorate and save the penitent, has become, by the servility of the Muscovite clergy, an instrument for spies for the benefit of the Czar; in fine, because the Synod has violated the law, and that its reforms are abitrary, and are made to further the objects of despotism. These acts of impiety being so notorious, and these truths so known, who shall now maintain that the Russian Church is not schismatic? Our Councils reject it, our canons forbid us to recognise it, our Church disowns it; and all who hold to the faith and whom she recognises for her children, are bound to respect her decision, and to consider the Russian rite a schismatic rite. Such are the motives which prevent the Roumains from attending the Russian Chapel in Paris." —(Quoted in *Blackwood's Magazine*, March, 1853.)

But even if they were of the same faith, the same hope, and acknowledged the same common headship as the Russian Greek Church, upon what right does Russia found her protectorate over these subjects of the Ottoman empire? The following are the three articles in the treaty of Kainardji which relate to the Turkish Greek subjects:—

"Article VII.—*The Porte* promises to protect the Christian religion and its churches; and the Ministers of Russia shall be allowed to make representations in favour of the new church of which mention is made in the 14th article.

"Article VIII.—The subjects of the Russian empire shall be permitted to visit the city of Jerusalem and the Holy Places; and no duty or contribution shall be exacted from them either at Jerusalem or elsewhere.

"Article XIV.—The Court of Russia is permitted, besides the chapel built in the Minister's house, to build in the quarter of Galata, in the street named Bey Oglou, a public church of the Greek rite, which shall always be under the protection of the Russian Minister, and secure from all vexation and exaction."—*(Blue Book*, vol. i., p. 51.)

Now this treaty states, as plainly as words can do, that *the Porte* is to protect the Christian religion and its churches, and that the protection of Russia is limited to the chapel to be built in the quarter of Galata, in the street named Bey Oglou: yet upon this treaty Russia claims her right to interfere, to occupy the Principalities for the purpose of obtaining material guarantees; and the Peace Society agrees to her claim and palliates, where it cannot justify, her acts.

Again, Mr. BRIGHT writes, "I have said nothing of the fact that all these troubles have sprung out of the demands made by France upon the Turkish Government, and urged in language more insulting than any which has been shown to have been used by Prince Menschikoff."—*(Letter*, pp. 13-14.) MR. THOMPSON, who appears to have made this letter the text for his various lucubrations, reiterates the same charge. Let us carefully examine this part of the subject. The claim of the French rests upon the treaty of 1740, which "vindicates the right of the Latins to an exclusive occupation of all the sanctuaries which they possessed at that time. The conferences lately opened here, have resulted in a clear establishment of that right as applied to the holy buildings—ten, I believe,

in number—most of which are now possessed jointly by the two communions, and some exclusively by the Greeks. M. de LAVALETTE, *instead of
pushing his right to an extreme, took upon himself the responsibility of
declaring his readiness to extend the principles of joint possession to the
whole number.* * * He (M. de LAVALETTE) has acted with moderation
throughout; he has been careful not to commit his Government—he has
made no written communication except his opening note and such documents as were necessary for establishing the joint commission of enquiry
—and he is anxious to act with moderation to the last; but at the same
time he thinks it impossible to submit with honour to the present plan of
proceeding; his Government, having embarked in the question, cannot,
with any degree of credit or consistency, stop short under the dictation of
Russia; the national party in France, the Catholic party there and elsewhere, will press for the full assertion of right under treaty—and, as for
himself, he will retire rather than be made the instrument, as he conceives
he would be, in the supposed case of his country's humiliation; nay more,
if it depended upon him, he would not hesitate to make use of the great
naval force now possessed by France in the Mediterranean, and by block-
ading the Dardanelles, bring the question in debate forthwith to a satisfactory issue."—*(Sir Stratford Canning to Viscount Palmerston, Nov.* 4,
1851; *Blue Book,* vol. i., p. 19.)

Those demands were supported by the plenipotentiaries of all the
Catholic Powers. England looked on without any personal interest in
the question itself; the Porte was anxious and unsettled, for Russia,
through M. de TITOFF, was loud in her demands for the *status quo,* and
threatened to leave Constantinople if it were disturbed. But this *status
quo* meant Russia's interpretation of it—meant, Russia being fully accepted as the Protector of the Greeks, which, as we saw, she strongly claimed
from the Hainardji Treaty; the *status quo* which France desired was simply
the restoration of rights which had been allowed to fall in abeyance by
the Latins, and had, in some measure, been acquired by the Greeks.

I do not state here how very trifling to us appear the causes which
led to those demands, because we cannot appreciate all this pother being
made about the possession of a key or two, the building of a cupola, and
the putting up of a silver star; but to the Latins such questions are of
great importance; and politically they served as indices to measure the
influence which the French and Russians exercised in the East. I pass
on to the official documents narrating the development of this quarrel.
Colonel ROSE, writing to the Earl of MALMESBURY, Nov. 20, 1852, says,
"A graver cause of difference than the great door of the Church of Bethlehem has appeared, and taken precedence of it.

"The Porte, under the influence of French and Russian menaces,
conceded to the French Embassy the note of the 9th February, and the
Firman of the Mi-Février to the Greeks.

"The Russian Government considers the Firman the Charter of Rights
of the Greek Church. The President and M. de LAVALETTE consider it
an affront to France, because it describes her claims, grounded on the
Treaty of 1740, as "haksig," unjust, and establishes a *status quo* which
wholly invalidates that Treaty. M. de LAVALETTE tells me that the
Porte promised to M. SABATIER that it should not be read at Jerusalem.

"M. D'OZEROFF tells the Porte that the Firman must be read at
Jerusalem; he declares that if it be not read, according to usage, in the·

Medgliss at Jerusalem, before the Pasha, Cadi, Members of the Council, Patriarchs of the different sects, it will be valueless and a dead letter, and that, consequently, faith will have been broken with Russia."—*(Blue Book,* vol. i., p. 46.)

This irritable state of things assumed a more amicable aspect by December 4, 1852: writing at that date, Colonel ROSE says, "M. de LAVA-LETTE now says that nothing can be more pleasant and amiable (plus doux et plus aimable) than he is with the Porte. I humbly and respectfully demand my right. (Je demande humblement et respecteusement mon droit). M. d'OZEROFF also says, that although he admitted that last year there had been a declaration that the Russian Legation would, under certain circumstances, leave Constantinople, yet, that he could not bring to his recollection having talked of the Legation leaving it on account of present causes of differences with the Porte.—*(Blue Book,* vol. i., pp. 49-50.)

While the question of the Holy Places was thus winding its weary way along, the Emperor of Russia was ordering troops to the frontiers of the Danubian Provinces. On the 4th of January, 1853, Sir G. H. SEY-MOUR writes to Lord JOHN RUSSELL, that " orders have been dispatched to the 5th corps d'armée to advance to the frontiers of the Danubian Provinces, *without waiting for their reserves;* and the 4th corps, under the command of General Count DANNENBERG, and now stationed in Volhynia, will be ordered to hold itself in readiness to march if necessary. Each of these corps consists of twenty-four regiments, and, as your Lordship is aware, each Russian regiment is composed of three battalions (each of about 1000 men), of which one battalion forms the reserve. General LUDER's corps d'armée accordingly, being now 48,000 strong, will receive a reinforcement of 24,000 men soon after its arrival at its destination, and supposing the 4th corps to follow, the whole force will amount at least, according to official returns, to 144,000 men."—*(Blue Book,* vol. i., p. 56)

January 28, 1853, Colonel ROSE says, " Both the French and Russian Representatives exhibit now most laudable moderation in the matter of the Holy Places."—*(Blue Book,* vol. i., p. 79.)

And now new events occur in this strange drama. The three great Powers—England, France, and Russia—remove their ambassadors and appoint new ones. England sent Viscount STRATFORD DE REDCLIFFE, France, M. de la COUR, and Russia, the notorious Prince MENCHIKOFF. The first act of the Russian officer was an insult to the Porte—an insult committed with intention, and at once indicating both the character of the mission and of the man appointed to execute it. Colonel ROSE writes to Lord JOHN RUSSELL, March 3, 1853, " A painful sensation was caused here by the following incident, which occurred yesterday :—Prince MEN-CHIKOFF paid his official visit to the Grand Vizier, at the Porte, but purposely omitted to pay it to FUAD EFFENDI, who was ready to receive him." —*(Blue Book,* vol. i., p. 85.)

In another despatch, dated March 7, 1853, are these passages :— "Circumstances connected with the mission of Prince MENCHIKOFF have gradually come to light, and cause grave apprehension for the independence, if not the destiny, of Turkey. * * Unfortunately, Prince MEN-CHIKOFF's first public act evinced *entire disregard, on his part, of the Sultan's dignity and rights, which, combined with the hostile attitude of*

Russia, created the impression that coercion, rather than conciliatory nego-tiation, would distinguish his Excellency's mission." And, further on, speaking of the affront offered to FUAD EFFENDI, he says, "The affront was the more galling, because great preparations had been made for the purpose of receiving the Russian Ambassador with marked honours, and a great concourse of people, particularly Greeks, had assembled for the pur-pose of witnessing the ceremony. The incident made a great and most painful sensation. The Grand Vizier expressed to me his indignation at the premeditated affront which had been offered to his Sovereign, and the Sultan's irritation was excessive. M. BENEDETTI and myself at once saw all the bearing and intention of the affront. *Prince* MENCHIKOFF *wished, at his first start, to create an intimidating or commanding influence—to show that any man, even a Cabinet Minister, who had offended Russia, would be humiliated and punished, even in the midst of the Sultan's Court, and without previous communication to His Majesty. Prince Menchikoff wished to take the cleverest man out of the Ministry, humiliate it, upset it, and establish in its place a Ministry favourable to his views, If this manœuvre had succeeded, a second treaty, like that of Unkier Skelessi, or something worse, would probably have been the result."—(Blue Book,* vol. i., pp. 86-7.

Such was the commencement of the mission of that man whose mode-ration Englishmen have been found prejudiced enough to praise. Nor can there be a doubt respecting the intention of Russia. While her Ambassador was insulting the Porte before the eyes of the assembled peo-ple, active preparations were being made to concentrate troops on the Danubian Provinces. Our Vice-Consul, CHARLES CUNNINGHAM, writing from Galatz, February 25, 1853, nearly two months before Prince MEN-CHIKOFF arrived at Constantinople, says, " For some months past, there have been rumours that a large Russian force has been collected in Bess-arabia, and even that these Provinces were to be occupied. From the information I have obtained, I consider it certain that the inhabitants of Bessarabia, in the districts around Ismail and Reni, have orders to pre-pare quarters for 60,000 troops."—(*Blue Book,* vol. i., p. 90). The French Consul at Jassy confirms this statement. He says: " All persons and letters coming from Bessarabia concur in saying that very serious preparations for war are there making—(s' accordent à dire qu'il s'y fait ce très-sérieux preparatifs de guerre). Vast supplies of biscuit are already prepared, and the troops have received orders to hold themselves in readi-ness to march at the first signal."—*(Blue Book,* vol. i., p. 92.) Yet amidst all this warlike preparation Russia still continued to talk of her "pacific intentions"—of her "desire to preserve the independence and integrity of the Ottoman empire"—of her " deep respect and friendly feelings towards His Majesty the Sultan." She manifested the truth of her words by sending an ambassador to insult, and concentrating troops to overawe, her dear friend, the Sultan, whose rights, more than her own, she hypocritically declared to be the great purpose at which she aimed.

This concentration of troops on the frontier, connected with the con-duct of Prince MENCHIKOFF at the Capital, naturally aroused the suspicion and called for the watchfulness of the other Powers. As Sir G. H. SEY-MOUR said to the Russian Chancellor, "if the presence of a Russian army on the borders of the Principalities is likely to arouse the apprehension of foreign Governments, what effects is it calculated to produce upon the

Porte?"—(*Blue Book*, vol. i., p. 58.) That effect was well calculated by Russia. She hoped to produce fear, disaffection, disturbance and bloodshed, in the midst of which she might come in as a protector, carry on her old and well-learnt tactics, and end in appropriating to her own colossal territories—the greater part acquired by fraud or war. It was her old plan. The world has been the almost indifferent spectator of her custom for more than sixty years. She now began in Turkey, as she began in Poland, in Finland, in Courland, in Georgia, in Bessarabia, and in every other country which her insatiable greed and ambition desired. Her process "has almost been reduced to a regular formula. It invariably commences with disorganization, by means of corruption and secret agency, pushed to the extent of disorder and civil contention. Next in order comes military occupation, to restore tranquility; and *in every instance the result has been* PROTECTION, *followed by* INCORPORATION."* But I anticipate.

The plot thickens as it proceeds. From a communication of M. PISANI's to Colonel ROSE, March 19, 1853, it appears that he "got information from good authority that this moderate behaviour on the part of the Russian Ambassador is calculated to induce the Porte to assent to the conclusion of a *secret compact.*"—*(Blue Book*, vol. i., p. 107.) Again, Colonel ROSE says, March 25, 1853, "The Grand Vizier informs me, also, that, in the projected treaty, there is a clause which could be interpreted into protection, by Russia, of the Turkish Greek Church."—*(Blue Book*, vol. i., pp. 107-8.) Yet we are told by the Peace Party that Russia asked for and demanded nothing but the preservation of the *status quo*; and, as we saw by the articles of the Treaty of Kainardji, such protection formed no part of the *status quo*.

During all these strange proceedings, and amid all these cross purposes, Prince MENCHIKOFF, true to his Russian policy, was silent as to the main object of his mission. He even "tried to exact a promise from RIFAAT PASHA, *before he makes known to him the nature of his mission and of his demands, that the Porte shall make a formal promise that she will not reveal them to the British or French Representatives.* RIFAAT PASHA declined, and Prince MENCHIKOFF declared that if the object of his mission was not promptly settled, *he must leave Constantinople;* but he modified this declaration by saying that he did not mean thereby to imply that his retirement would be the signal for war."—*(Blue Book*, vol. i., p. 109.)

In order that no mistake may be made respecting the object of Prince MENCHIKOFF's mission, I quote from the note of M. DORIA to Colonel ROSE, dated April 1, 1853, the following passage:—"Prince MENCHIKOFF had verbally expressed the Emperor's wish to enter into a secret treaty with Turkey, *putting a fleet and* 400,000 *men at her disposal, if she ever needed aid against any Western Power whatever.* That Russia further secretly demanded an addition to the treaty of Kainardji, whereby the Greek Church should be placed *entirely under Russian protection, without reference to Turkey,* which was to be the equivalent for the preferred aid above mentioned."—*(Blue Book*, vol. i., p. 112.) While these interferences with the rights of the Ottoman Porte were systematically pursued at Constantinople, Russia was busily employed in the same insidious course in Servia. Lord CLARENDON informs Lord STRATFORD DE RED-

* The Progress and Present Position of Russia in the East: an Historical Summary, Preface, p. vi.

B

CLIFFE, April 18, 1853, that "the Prince of Servia has dismissed M. GARASCHANIN from his service, on the *peremptory demand of Prince Menchikoff*, and that the Russian Consul at Belgrade has subsequently, in threatening terms, required the removal of several other official persons. This interference with the internal government of the Province has excited much discontent among the Servian people; and your Excellency is instructed to state to Prince MENCHIKOFF, that in the opinion of Her Majesty's Government, a perseverance in this course will be productive of mischievous results."—*(Blue Book,* vol. i., p. 122.)

Can any sane man doubt the object of all this interference, the purpose of all these threatenings, and the aim of all this diplomatic bullying and intrigue? The original causes assigned by Russia for such interference had been removed; and, as Colonel ROSE told Prince MENCHIKOFF, "the recall of M. de LAVALETTE and the retirement of FUAD EFFENDI must be considered a satisfactory reparation; that Montenegro had been evacuated; that, in short, none of the causes alleged by Russia as causes for a hostile attitude existed any longer."—(vol. i., p. 122.)

By May 6, 1853, the subject of the Holy Places was settled, both to the satisfaction of M. de la COUR and Prince MENCHIKOFF; when, having received fresh instructions from Russia, Prince MENCHIKOFF sent a decisive communication to the Porte; concerning which Sir STRATFORD DE REDCLIFFE says, "it must appear the more alarming to the Porte, as it has followed close upon his Excellency's receipt of the *firmans and official note which but yesterday terminated with his assent the question of the Holy Places.* That communication is, moreover, peremptory in fixing a very brief delay for the Porte's definitive reply; and it comprises the Russian *note verbale* of the 19th ultimo in its more formal expression of Russia's demands. It insists in certain unexplained additions to the settlement of the Jerusalem question, but little palatable to France; and although in some degree moderated in comparison with its original extent, requires, under the name of 'guarantee,' a concesson, the dangerous character of which will not escape your Lordship's observation."—(Vol i., p. 164.) Prince MENCHIKOFF's words are, "the Ambassador begs his Excellency, RIFAAT PASHA, to be good enough to let him have that answer by Tuesday next, May 10. He cannot consider a longer delay in any other light than as a want of respect towards his Government, *which would* impose upon him the most painful duty."—(Vol. i., p. 167.)

We have now reached a point of the present discussion at which we may pause, and sum up the result. It appears from the passages quoted from the various despatches of different ambassadors, that though the French were the first introducers of the question of the Holy Places, the quarrel, so far as they were concerned, was now satisfactorily and amicably settled. That they might have been to blame in the first instance, scarcely affects the after development of the plans and projects of Russia. M. de la COUR was satisfied, Prince MENCHIKOFF was, or said he was, satisfied, the French Government authorised M. de la COUR "to state that, with regard to the question of the Holy Places," she was "satisfied. The present arrangement is the arrangement made by M. de LAVALETTE, and France has consequently nothing to say against it. M. de la COUR is enjoined neither to protest nor to make reserves."—*(Blue Book,* vol. i, p. 175.) Yet this very moment of apparently amicable arrangement is chosen by Russia to make other claims, and to demand other privileges; then it was that Russia sent in her *ulti-*

matum, and sought to exercise the power of a virtual sovereign over 11,000,000 of Turkish subjects, the vast majority of whom dread nothing more than the exercise of such authority, and who have shown, during the present contest, how earnest they are in repelling the assumptions of the Emperor of Russia. In Servia "the great majority are patriotic and desirous to exclude all extraneous intervention in their affairs. They are content with their present position and connexion with Turkey, which strengthens without annoying them."* So it is with the other Provinces over which Russia seeks to spread the terrible power of her protection. Her protection is degradation, debasement, and oppression. She has no scruples, for she worships a policy. Whatever may help to develope that policy, be it lying, intrigue, rebellion, spoliation, violation of Treaties, or even murder and assassination, are resorted to. Nothing intimidates her— nothing turns her aside. Rebuffed now, she bides her time, and then makes another attempt, to be succeeded by another, and another, and another, if necessary for the accomplishment of her object. She talks of her good faith at the same moment she is violating some solemnly-sworn contract; she invokes the person and aid of Almighty God in all her undertakings, though of the blackest and basest kind. It has been well said that the "kind of faith with which she has acted is shown in the revolts she has instigated and sustained in so many Turkish Provinces while she was at peace with the Sultan and professing the warmest friendship. The *good faith* of Russia is that which she exhibits in not less than twenty-one schools of Bulgaria, where the Russians from Kiew—the Mecca of the Muscovites—teach the children who are all Turkish subjects. hatred of the Sultan as a part of their religious instruction, and submission to the Czar as necessary to their eternal salvation."† Such is her protection—such has it ever been; and by this insidious conduct she is every year adding or preparing for future additions to her ill-gotten possessions. But we are told that "the seat of war is 3,000 miles away from us. We had not been attacked—not even insulted in any way;"§ and therefore we ought to have had nothing to do with the quarrel. No matter that existing Treaties between ourselves and Turkey declare that we ought to interfere; no matter that the future safety and honour of Europe—probably of England herself—depended upon the course we took in this question; no matter that right, justice, and truth were on the side of Turkey; and wrong, insolence, and unwarrantable aggression on the part of Russia; "the seat of war is 3,000 miles away from us" and—we had nothing to do with the quarrel. Happily the Government and the people took a different view of the subject, and opposed the great enemy.

Prince MENCHIKOFF left Constantinople May 23rd, 1853. Mr. BRIGHT has the following curious passage: "But for the English Minister at Constantinople and the Cabinet at home, the dispute would have settled itself. and the last note of Prince MENCHIKOFF would have been accepted; and no human being can point out any material difference between that note and the Vienna note afterwards agreed upon and recommended by the Governments of England, France, Austria, and Prussia. But our Government would not allow the dispute to be settled." It would be difficult to select any passage in the whole range of English literature, of a similar

* Progress of Russia in the East: an Historical Summary, p. 153.
† Progress of Russia in the East: an Historical Summary, p. 159.
§ Letter of JOHN BRIGHT, Esq., M.P.

length, containing so many sophisms as this. The note of Prince MEN-CHIKOFF was so indentical with the Vienna note, that the Porte rejected both. And instead of the English Ambassador preventing the amicable arrangement of the question, he, acting under instructions from home, exerted every means, short of cowardice and dishonour, to preserve the peace. Passage upon passage could be selected from the Blue Book, from despatches of Lord PALMERSTON, of the Earl of MALMESBURY, of Lord JOHN RUSSELL, of the Earl of CLARENDON, from the letters of Colonel ROSE and Lord STRATFORD de RELCLIFFE, illustrative of this statement; and, because the Sultan was advised not to accede to a demand which would have destroyed his authority over 11,000,000 of his subjects, England is charged with not allowing the dispute to be settled ; and because the Vienna note only reiterated MENCHIKOFF'S *ultimatum,* this attempt to produce peace met the same fate as the others ; still it is England that prevented the settlement of the dispute. For we are told that " Prince MENCHIKOFF, in his note dated the 21st of May, which has caused a profound impression throughout Europe, has proclaimed that religious objects alone have not been aimed at by him."—*(Blue Book,* vol. i., p. 268.) Russia now pursued her usual course. She issued a Manifesto, June 26, 1853;—a copy of this Manifesto was published in the "St. Petersburgh Journal,"—and this Manifesto differed essentially from the Manifesto issued to the Russian people. "Considerable sensation," says Sir G. H. SEYMOUR, "has been occasioned among the Foreign Missions at St. Petersburgh, by the great differences observable in the Russian manifesto as published in its original state, that is, as addressed to the Russian people, and in the official French translation destined for more general circulation in the 'St. Petersburgh Journal.' "

The most striking word in the original was "perfidiousness," as applied to the Sultan, an epithet which the Government translator appears to have been desired to omit.

I need not observe, that the suppression is calculated to give an erroneous general impression of the force of that appeal which the Emperor's Government has judged it necessary to make to the prejudices—for, in this instance, I will not say opinions—of the Russian people.—*(BlueBook* vol. i., p. 340.) This manifesto contained this passage :—" Having exhausted all persuasion and, with them, every means of obtaining pacific satisfaction of our just demands, *we have found it needful to advance our armies into the Danubian Principalities, in order to show the Ottoman Porte to what its obstinacy may lead.*"*—(Blue Book,* vol. i., p. 323.) Of course, this never meant war—of course, these acts were the legitimate consequences of the Emperor's continued assertion of his desire for peace, and his intentions of preserving the integrity of the Ottoman Empire. This pacific course was only for the purpose of possessing a "material guarantee," and was not a *casus belli.* The Western Powers were foolish enough so to consider it ; and Turkey was persuaded not to declare war when it occurred, because the very power which Mr. BRIGHT says was the cause why the quarrel could not be amicably settled, had not yet given up the

---

* " Now the Principalities have been invaded, not only without any pretence of right, but by the most flagrant violations of all the principles of right, by the armies of Russia, The revenues of the Principalities have been seized, all the private *material* of those countries sequestered, and the inhabitants compelled to join the Russian armies and to make war on their own Sovereign."—*Lord Lyndhurst, in the House of Lords, March 20,* 1855. Even weak, vacillating, and Russia-allied Prussia was forced to admit that " a great wrong had been committed."

hope of her ability to procure peace. The Russians crossed the Pruth, issued their manifesto which was in the stereotype style of all the manifestos which, under similar circumstances, she has issued during the last sixty years—issued to deceive Europe, and not as indices of her conduct. This is the manifesto:—

"Inhabitants of Moldavia and Wallachia! His Majesty the Emperor of Russia, my august master has commanded me to occupy your territory with the corps d'armée, of which he has been pleased to confide to me the command.

"We arrive among you neither with plans of conquest nor with the intention of modifying the institutions by which you are governed, or the political situation guaranteed to you by solemn Treaties.

"The provisional occupation of the Principalities which I am directed to carry out, has no other object than that of immediate and effectual protection in the unlooked-for and ruinous circumstances under which the Ottoman Government, disregarding the numerous proofs of a sincere alliance which the Imperial Court, since the conclusion of the treaty of Adrianople, has never ceased to give it, responds to our most just proposals by refusals, to our most disinterested advice by the most offensive distrust.

"In his longanimity, in his constant desire to maintain peace in the East as well as in Europe, the Emperor will avoid engaging in an offensive war against Turkey, so long as his dignity and the interests of his Empire will permit him to do so.

"On the very day that he shall obtain the reparation which is due to him, and the guarantee which he is entitled to require for the future, his troops will withdraw within the frontiers of Russia.

"Inhabitants of Moldavia and Wallachia! I equally execute an order of His Imperial Majesty, by declaring to you that the presence of his troops in your country will not impose upon you either fresh charges or contributions; that the supplies of provisions will be paid for by our military chests at a suitable time, and at a rate fixed beforehand in concert with your Governments.

"Look upon what awaits you without disquietude; betake yourselves in security to your agricultural labours and to your commercial speculations; obey the laws which govern you, and the constituted authorities. By the faithful discharge of these duties you will acquire the best title to the generous solicitude and powerful protection of His Majesty the Emperor."—(Blue Book, vol. i., pp. 348-9.)

This is the usual course of Russian invasions. She burglariously takes possession of territory, and tells the people that if they will be quiet and obedient, they shall receive the "generous solicitude" of the imperial robber. All her proclamations are similar to this in word, identical in purpose, and observed with the same supreme indifference. For the reader's information I will quote a passage from the proclamation published in 1808, upon the invasion of Finland; it will be seen that it is written in the same spirit, and was carried out with the same fidelity:—"It is with the greatest regret that his Majesty the Emperor of Russia, &c., sees himself forced to send into your country the troops under my order. * * These motives, as well as the regard which his Imperial Majesty owes to the safety of his own states, oblige him to place your country under his protection, and to take possession of it, in order to procure by these means a sufficient guarantee in case his Swedish Majesty should persevere in his resolution not to accept the equitable conditions of peace that have been proposed to him. * * It is his Imperial Majesty's pleasure that all the affairs of the country should have their ordinary course in conformity with your laws and customs, which will remain in force so long as his Imperial Majesty's troops shall be obliged to occupy the country. The civil and military functionaries are confirmed in their respective employments; always excepting those who may use their authority to mislead the people, and induce them to take measures contrary to their interests. All that is necessary for the maintenance and food of the troops shall be paid in ready money on the spot. All provisions shall be paid for according to an amicable agreement between our commissaries and those of the country." A passage from the letter of the King of Sweden will show how these promises are kept. He says, "Honour and humanity require me to make strong representations against the innumerable horrors and the vexations which the Russian troops have permitted themselves in Swedish Finland. The blood of the innocent victims calls for vengeance upon those who authorised such cruelties. * * * Can it be a crime in my Finnish subjects not to have wished to let themselves be seduced by promises which are as fallacious as the principles on which they are founded are erroneous! Is it worthy of a Sovereign to make it in them a crime? I conjure your Imperial Majesty to put an end to the calamities and the horrors of a war which ought to call down on your person and your empire the malediction of Divine Providence."* We know that Finnish protection ended in Incorporation, and, but for the glorious bravery of the Turks at Oltenitza, Citate, and Silistria, and the interference of the Allies, such would, without doubt, have been the fate of the Principalities. The same tactics were employed; similar oppressions exercised; identical courses pursued. Russia ordered the taxes to be paid to her general; required obedience from the Hospadas and service from the people; forbade their communicating with the Sultan, their lawful ruler. This general order will shew what kind of protection she exercised: "Ordered 1st. That all men from the age of eighteen to forty years, married or unmarried, and whatever their profession may be, are required by the generals, colonels, and commanders of corps to do service for the Russian army. 2. That horses, waggons, oxen, and other beasts of burden, may be required for the same service. And, 3. That all boats, barks, or floats now on the Danube, are seized for the present moment for the service of the Russian army. This decree is applicable to all Wallachian subjects. Those who attempt to evade its execution shall *be tried by court martial.*" Such is Russian protection.

We now reach the period of the famous Vienna note, which, says Mr. BRIGHT, "Russia accepted at once—accepted it, I believe, by telegraph, even before the precise words of it had been received in St. Petersburgh. Everybody thought the question now settled. A Cabinet Minister told me we should never hear another word about it; 'the whole thing is at an end,' he said, and so it appeared for a moment. But the Turk refused the note which had been drawn up by his own arbitrators, and which Russia had accepted." No one will be surprised at the Turk rejecting this note, when he reads the original words of the note and compares them with the suggested amendments of the Ottoman Government:

---

* Progress of Russia in the East: an Historical Summary, pp. 148-49.

If the Emperors of Russia have at all times evinced their active solicitude for *the maintenance of the immunities and privileges of the orthodox Greek Church in the Ottoman Empire, the Sultans have never refused again to confirm them* by solemn acts testifying their ancient and constant benevolence towards their Christian subjects.

His Majesty the Sultan will remain faithful *to the letter and to the spirit of the Treaties of Kainardji and Adrianople, relative to the protection of the Christian religion,* * * * and moreover in a spirit of exalted equity, to cause the Greek rite to share in the advantages *granted to the other Christian rites by Convention or special arrangement.*

If the Emperors of Russia have at all times evinced their active solicitude for *the religion and orthodox Greek Church, the Sultans have never ceased to provide for the maintenance of the privileges and immunities which at different times they have spontaneously granted to that religion and to that Church in the Ottoman Empire, and to confirm them.*

His Majesty the Sultan will remain faithful *to the stipulations of the Treaty of Kainardji, confirmed by that of Adrianople relative to the protection by the Sublime Porte of the Christian religion, and he is moreover charged to make known,* * * * and moreover in a spirit of exalted equity, to cause the Greek rite to share in the advantages *granted, or which might be granted, to the other Christian Communities, Ottoman subjects.*

The intellect which cannot see the difference—the essential difference—of these words must, in some way or other, be very far from being healthy. The three great Powers acknowledged the justice of the alterations, and M. Drouyn de Lhuys, though he "regrets the introduction of any modifications into the Vienna note, certainly considers them to be for the better."—*(Blue Book,* vol. ii., p. 85.) These modifications the Emperor of Russia refused to accept; and though France and England, still desirous of peace, advised the Turks not to declare war against Russia, is it surprising that she did? The wonder is that she suffered her hands to be tied so long, considering that the enemy was in her territories and exercising all the powers of military government over her subjects. Because Turkey refused the first note, and Russia the amended one, Mr. Bright has the audacity to tell us that "the Turks should have been prevented from going to war, *or should have been allowed to go to war on their own risk.*" In no fit of temporary excitement did the Turks adopt this last resort of nations. She summoned a council of her wisest, her gravest, and her best, and then, after mature deliberation, issued the declaration of war. "The decisions were unanimous. The meeting consisted of more than a hundred persons."—*(Blue Book,* vol. ii., p. 130.)

Such is the history of that contest which is at present waging between England, France, Turkey, and Russia. I have endeavoured to state the whole question without prejudice or passion. Believing thoroughly in the justice of the war, I have sought to master all its bearings, and so to state the result that reason should be the only adjudicator appealed to. I have expressed few opinions of my own, preferring to quote from official documents, so that the reader might have the authoritative documents in his possession, and be thus enabled to compare them with the garbled extracts which have been made from these very interesting Blue Books on the Holy Places. The whole development of the question reveals Russia at her old game; a game she has unceasingly played since the time of Peter I.; a game by which she has more than doubled her original empire; a game which has brought to her unholy rule Poland, Finland, the Crimea, Georgia, Bessarabia, and so many other provinces which she has filched from her neighbours. "For one hundred and sixty years Russia has steadily kept in view the objects of ambition in the East first contemplated by Peter I., and bequeathed by him to his successors. These were, to raise Russia upon the ruins of Turkey—to obtain exclusive possession of the Caspian and Black Sea, with the Bosphorus and the Dardanelles—to extend her dominions beyond the Caucasus—to domineer in Persia with a view to open the road to India; and history perhaps furnishes no other example of equal pertinacity in prosecuting, *per fas et nefas*, a predetermined course of aggrandisement. Her crown has frequently been transferred, by open violence or secret crime, from one head or one family to another, but each successive sovereign, with hardly an exception, has made some progress towards the attainment of these objects, and she continues to prosecute them with unabated avidity."* Yet, with these facts before his eyes, and strengthening himself with a quotation from Lord PALMERSTON, who says just what suits his purpose at the moment, Mr. BRIGHT declares that " The danger of the Russian power was a phantom." Any one might suppose from such statements that men read history with their understandings warped by some strange hallucination which prevented them from profitting by its lessons. Russian power of aggression a phantom ! Why her whole modern history is one continued record of aggressions committed on foreign states, and she is now as desirous as ever of increasing her dominions. The late Emperor was scarcely cold before his son, ALEXANDER II., asked "Providence which has selected us for so high a calling to be our guide and protector, that we may maintain Russia on the highest standard of power and glory, and in our person accomplish the incessant wishes and aims of Peter, of Catherine, of Alexander, and of our father." One of these incessant wishes and aims is the possession of Constantinople, the Bosphorous, and the Dardanelles.

To show the nature of the Russian policy and her unvarying method of carrying it out, I select a few instances of her aggressions. A goodly volume might be filled with such violations of all rights, natural and divine:—From Sweden she gained Finland in 1809 ; the lion's share of Poland fell to her after the three fatal partitions of 1772, 1793, and 1795, and Warsaw was added in 1815; from Persia she wrung Georgia, in 1814 ; and Turkey lost the Crimea in 1784, and Bessarabia in 1812. I now give an abstract of the extent of her acquisitions, which proves that within the last sixty-four years she has acquired territories equal in extent and importance to the whole empire she had in Europe before that time. From Sweden she has stolen more than what now remains of that kingdom ; what she won from Poland nearly equals the whole Austrian empire ; from Turkey in Europe, her gain is greater than the Prussian dominions, exclusive of the Rhenish Provinces ; and from Turkey in Asia it is nearly equal to the whole of the smaller states of Germany. Persia has been plundered of dominions equal to England ; and from Tartary she has filched possessions not inferior to that of Turkey in Europe, Greece, Italy, and Spain.† Surely this is a sufficient evidence of her aggressive policy, and also sufficient to show that her power is not a mere phantom.

Mr. BRIGHT can never have read Russian history, or he would scarcely have penned the sentence that we are at war for " the mainte-

---

* The Progress of Russia in the East : an Historical Summary. Preface, pp. v. and vi.
† The above abstract is made from Mr. ARROWSMITH's valuable map, accompanying the pamphlet, " The Progress of Russia in the East ; an Historical Summary.

nance of the most immoral and filthy of all despotisms over one of the fairest portions of the earth which it has desolated, and over a population it has degraded, but has not been able to destroy." Bad as Turkish despotism has been, it must pale its ineffectual fires before that of Russia; the horrors committed by Peter and Catherine, the religious persecutions of Nicholas, the fate of the Minsk nuns, the massacre of thousands of unopposing and helpless victims which everywhere defiles her annals. Of her horrible crimes, too hideous to be named; of her serf population, of her degraded priesthood guilty of every enormity of which human nature is capable, I need not here enlarge. From the days when Peter had his own son assassinated, butchered his people, massacred the Strelitzes, and at a banquet which he gave to the Prussian Ambassador, Prinz, had twenty of these unfortunate men brought into the room and there beheaded; and as each head fell he quaffed a bumper, desiring his guest to do the same; from the days when her Generals POTEMKIN and SUVAROFF, at the command of Catherine, slaughtered in the Crimea "thirty thousand Tartars of either sex and every age, in cold blood," down to the Sinope horrors of last year, her policy, her spirit, her objects and aims have undergone no change. And it is sad quibbling to say, as it has recently been said by an advocate of the Peace Society, that the Secret Correspondence contains not a single word threatening, or intimating a threat, of active aggression on the part of Russia against the "sick man." Russia never *talks* of active aggression, but always of peace, and is always aggrandising. Her course is well drawn by her own historian KARAMSIN, and he says, "The object and character of our military policy has invariably been, *to seek to be at peace with everybody, and to make conquests without war; always keeping ourselves on the defensive, placing no faith on the friendship of those whose interests do not accord with our own, and losing no opportunity of injuring, without ostensibly breaking our treaties with them.*" Such is the moral code of a nation whose apologists are not a few in free and moral England!

The Emperor tells Europe, and Mr. BRIGHT supports him, that "England and France have sided with the enemies of Christianity against Russia combating for the Orthodox Faith." Now if the Turks have justice on their side, and I trust sufficient evidence has been advanced to prove they have, how can we be at war against Christianity in supporting them? Is not justice the very basis of all religion? It is the basis and only true ground-work of mercy itself, without which it is mere idleness to talk of religion. But the Czar and Mr. BRIGHT have availed themselves of the simple fact that the Russians *profess* Christianity, and that the Turks are Mahommedans, to inform the world that we are fighting the battle of the infidel against the faithful. We will not pause here to show what a Christianity this is which the Emperor proclaims as the only one orthodox faith, and for the propagation and establishment of which Russia has been selected by Divine Providence. It is not a religious war at all. It is simply a political war. But even if it were a religious war—by taking whose side in this quarrel should we be best helping the cause of religion? "Well," says a member of the Prussian Senate, "the *wrong* that Russia was doing was not made *right* by the religious grounds that she put forward as a pretence for her policy. It was true the question had a religious bearing; the whole earth was eventually to be converted to Christianity; but this providential future development of the world will not auth   se any one

c

secular power to constitute itself the executioner of the Divine will, and it could not be in conformity therewith when a great power sought to crush a weaker by a breach of treaty and force of arms." The Earl of SHAFTES-BURY, whose religious character none will doubt, and whose devotion to the cause of Religious Freedom has won for him a high place in the annals of England, has met this question in its true bearing. In his masterly speech in the House of Lords on the Turkish difficulty he said, "As to the alliance with Turkey, there is a wide difference between an alliance with any power, heathen though it may be, to maintain the cause of justice and order against the aggressions of professing Christians, and an alliance of which the result would be the development and aggrandisement of that power. Justice, Order, and Right are such things in the eyes of God that they must be respected * * It could be shown that, with the Turks, there were facilities for the promotion of civilization and the improvement of mankind, which were denied to the Christians within the territory of Russia, and which would be still more denied them if the Emperor were enabled to extend his dominions over the East. There are more than forty towns and villages in Turkey in which there are distinct congregations of Protestant seceders from the Greek Church. * * During the last twenty years the diffusion of the Bible in Turkey had been almost incredible ; whereas not even a single copy had been printed in Russia—the language of the people since 1823, and the circulation of it is forbidden under the severest penalties. With a population of 2,000,000 of Jews in his dominions, the Emperor will not permit a single copy of the Scriptures in Hebrew to pass the frontiers." The Earl of SHAFTESBURY also read the following Imperial Firman, which shows the liberality of the Sultan in strong contrast to the persecuting spirit of the Czar :—

"FIRMAN.—To my Vizier, Mahmoud Pasha, Prefect of Police in Constantinople. When this sublime and august mandate reaches you, let it be known that hitherto those of my Christian subjects who have embraced the Protestant faith have suffered much inconvenience and distress. But, in necessary accordance with my Imperial compassion, which is the support of all, and which is manifested to all classes of my subjects, it is contrary to my Imperial pleasure that any one class of them should be exposed to suffering. As, therefore, by reason of their faith, the above-mentioned are already a separate community, it is my Royal compassionate will that, for facilitating the conducting of their affairs, and that they may obtain ease, and quiet, and safety, a faithful and trustworthy person from among themselves, and by their own selection, shall be appointed, with the title of *Agent for the Protestants*, and that he should be in relations with the Prefecture of the Police. You will not permit anything to be required of them in the name of fee, or other pretence, for marriage licences or registration. You will see to it, that, like the other communities of the empire, in all their affairs, such as procuring cemeteries and places of worship, they should have every facility and every needful assistance. You will not permit that any of the other communities shall in any way interfere with their edifices, or with their worldly matters or concerns, or, in short, with any of their affairs, either secular or religious, that thus they may be free to exercise the usages of their faith. And it is enjoined upon you not to allow them to be molested an iota in these particulars, or in any others ; and that all attention and perseverance be put in requisition to maintain them in quiet and security. And, in case of necessity, they shall be free to make representations regarding their affairs, through their agent, to the Sublime Porte."

" In this," continued the Earl, " I believe is to be found the whole secret of the movement on the part of the Emperor of Russia. He saw that it would give to these Greek Christians a status, a recognized independence, and emancipated them from the influence of Russia; he saw that the circulation of the Scriptures was giving rise to those aspirations after liberty, which religious freedom must inevitably be followed by, and his own dominions were contiguous to those in which this religious freedom was tolerated."

The true nature of Russia's religious movement is well pointed out by Lord STRATFORD de REDCLIFFE. He is giving the Earl of CLARENDON a summary of the state of the question when he arrived at Constantinople, and of the difficulties which lie in the way of its settlement. As respects arriving at an amicable adjustment of the differences he says, " The prospect in this direction would be more promising if Russia were to shew signs of being disposed to act on Christian rather than on sectarian principles. But it appears that the protection which her Government wish to exercise with so little control or limitation, is of a strictly exclusive character; and it has reached me, from more quarters than one, that, among the motives for increasing their influence in this country, is the desire of repressing Protestantism wherever it appears."—(Blue Book, vol. i., p. 29.)

England, France, and Turkey have striven to divest this quarrel of any character of Islamism versus Christianity, and to rest it on the broad basis of justice and right. The Emperor has sought to make it a second crusade, and has used every influence in his power as head of the Church to excite the fanaticism, sectarian zeal, and religious bigotry of his people. In doing so he has shown himself capable of calling into action the most terrible of all weapons, so that therewith he can achieve his end. It was little to have been expected that a member of the most peaceful and tolerant of Christian communities should have aided him in this dreadful and iniquitous course. It is one more fatal illustration of how far men will allow themselves to be carried when once they abandon the strict path of reason, and allow feeling and prejudice to warp their otherwise sound judgment.

Before I leave this question of the " secret correspondence," I will quote a passage from Sir G. H. SEYMOUR, which I commend to the most careful consideration of those who think that Russia was desirous of keeping on terms of amity and justice with the Porte. The words are,—"The sovereign who insists with much pertinacity upon the impending fall of a neighbouring state, must have settled in his own mind that the hour, if not *of* its dissolution, yet *for* its dissolution, is at hand." To my mind, it is clear in what manner NICHOLAS had made up his mind respecting this dissolution; and it was no fault of his if the hour is not at hand.

A few words more. One course pursued by the Peace Society is very strange. While apologising for and defending Russia, most of its public speakers and lecturers denounce France and Austria. I shall not defend either of these Powers. Those who oppose Russia on the same grounds which I do, will be slow to do *that*. But how can these men, opposing the present war, reconcile it to their consciences to seek to embroil us with two other powers? Is it that they only deprecate war when waged against a favourite despot, and are reckless as to fanning the flames when others are concerned? Whatever may be their reasons, it is still a strange problem—one which these gentlemen may find some difficulty in solving. Now that we are at war, let us hope that we shall not again sheath the sword until we have secured peace on such a firm and secure basis that it shall not be in the power of future squabblers about a key, a stone, or a cupola, on the one hand—nor of agrandising and unscrupulous ambition on the other—to overthrow the peace of nations, to threaten the existence and liberties of weaker states, to interrupt the commerce of the world, and to retard the civilization of the race. For many years Russia has been the incubus of Europe. She has laid her cold grasp upon all its aspirations, and sent out her serried legions to quench in blood the budding life and reviving freedom of many states. Her name has been a terror—her presence a curse; her instruments are fraud, rapine, and destruction; her rule is based upon ignorance, superstition and slavery; and, brutal herself, she knows of only one system of governing men—a system which depends on chains, the knout, Siberia, and death! The man who lands such a system is hardly fit to speak the tongue which Shakspere spoke; and, as he is so much of a Russian subject, it is a pity that his citizenship is not complete, and that he were a dweller beneath her mild rule—a sojourner beneath her clement skies. For him our forefathers have lived, fought, and achieved freedom in vain.

" Who would not blush, if such a man there be?
Who would not weep, if Atticus were he ?"

J. A. LANGFORD, PRINTER, ANN-STREET, BIRMINGHAM.

THE WAR;

ITS ORIGIN AND ITS CONSEQUENCES.

BY THE

RIGHT REV. HORATIO SOUTHGATE, D.D.

BISHOP OF THE PROTESTANT EPISCOPAL CHURCH IN AMERICA.

———•———

"Woe unto the world because of offences! for it must needs be that offences come; but woe to that man by whom the offence cometh."— MATTHEW xviii. 7.

———•———

LONDON:

JAMES MADDEN, 8, LEADENHALL STREET.

—

1855.

INTRODUCTION.

THE following review of the present dispute between Russia and Turkey, and of the policy of England and France in interfering, is from the pen of Bishop Southgate, of the American Protestant Episcopal Church. It appeared in parts, in the columns of three consecutive numbers of the CHURCHMAN, an American newspaper published in New York in the months of March and April last, and was stated to be the substance of a lecture on the Oriental Question, which the Right Rev. Prelate was prevented, by a domestic affliction, from delivering.

Bishop Southgate, as an American, cannot at least be charged with allowing himself to be swayed in the matter by *national* prejudice or partiality. For many years a resident in Turkey, he had singular opportunities of observing the mode of its government and the condition of its diversified populations; and, on the other hand, himself a citizen of a republican state, he can hardly be suspected of preference for a despotic rule like that of Russia. If his preposessions could have biassed his judgment, they surely would naturally have led him to take the side of England. The Bishop's views, therefore, of this unhappy quarrel, and his fears for its probable consequences to mankind, may be well worth the perusal of Englishmen, who, as a nation, are perhaps more deeply interested in the present struggle and its issue, than any other people in the world.

Approaching the question in regard to both sides, apart from political or national bias, the Bishop could have no object in view but the setting forth of the truth—the burden of his Heavenly Master's message—when he publicly delivered to his fellow-citizens in the United States the following statement of his views.

London, Nov. 16th, 1854,

THE WAR;

ITS ORIGIN AND ITS CONSEQUENCES.

IN order to understand the question at issue between
the Empires of Russia and Turkey, we must go back
through a period of 300 years. It was originally a question, not between a Christian and a Mohammedan power,
but between the two great branches of the Christian
Church, the Oriental and the Western, or rather the Greek
and the Latin. I will not go into a full sketch of the history of the controversy respecting the Holy Places, as the
scenes of our SAVIOUR'S life and sufferings in and about
Jerusalem are called. It will be enough for my present
purpose, to indicate that from the time when HELENA and
her son, CONSTANTINE the Great, built the church of the
Holy Sepulchre at Jerusalem, and that of the Nativity at
Bethlehem, until now, the guardianship of those sacred
shrines, and of others that have since risen in hardly less
memorable localities, has been, at different periods, harshly,
not to say fiercely, contested between the Greeks and Latins.
At one time the Latins held possession of them for a long
interval. At another, by treaty between FRANCIS I. and
SULEIMAN the Magnificent, they were placed under the
protection of France; and at another, by capitulations between the Sultan and LOUIS XIV., they were restored to
that protection. This seems to have been in 1673 In
1757, they were brought back to the Greeks; and I cannot
discover that any change has been made from that time till
the year 1850. There can be no reasonable question that
they belong of right to the Eastern Church, both because their original foundation was Oriental, and because
they fall within the Dioceses of Oriental Bishops. But the

question has never ceased to be a bone of contention between the Greeks and the Latins, even when treaties and
conventions had clearly, for the time being, vested the
guardianship in one or the other.   In LOUIS PHILIPPE'S
reign, an attempt was made to settle these disputed claims;
but it was interrupted by the Syrian war of 1840, and was
not resumed till 1850.   Then, by commission from LOUIS
NAPOLEON, at that time President of France, the Marquis
de LAVALETTTE proceeded to Constantinople, via Rome,
with instructions to demand the definite restoration of the
guardianship of several of the most important of the Holy
Places to the Latin Church.   I cannot explain the extraordinary conduct of the Porte under those circumstances,
without letting my reader into the secret of its habitual
policy towards the European Powers; and this I will do in
the words of an eminent official of the Ottoman Government,
himself a Christian, which he once used to me on an occasion,
when a matter of great importance to the interests of our
Church in the East was under discussion.   ' If you would
have,' he said, ' a thread to guide you through all the laby-
rinth of Turkish policy, you must take this single fact : The
invariable rule of the Porte, in all its dealings with the
European Powers, and even in its professed reforms at
home, is to stand 'well with Europe.   It has no other principle of action.   Dependent as it is on these powers for its
preservation, for its very life, it sacrifices everything to its
European reputation.   Hence those unmeasured efforts, paid
for by the Porte itself, to give it a good name in the European Press.   You have no true statement of things in your
newspapers.   The facts are created, or at least put into
shape, here, according to the pleasure of the Turkish Government.   Here they are poured into the French and
English Gazettes, and hence they percolate into your
American Journals.   It is all made up for the Western
market, and in this way you seldom learn the real condition
of things.'   I believe this statement to be a true one;
because it entirely accords with my own experience and observation, during a residence of fourteen years in Turkey.

It follows, from this view, that the system of the Turkish Government is a system of patchwork. There are no homogeneous principles running through it. At one time a rent occurs in some vexatious question which has arisen between it and some European Power. On such an occasion, the Porte does not go back to any first principle. It covers up the rent with the first convenient patch that is at hand. It accommodates itself to the necessities of the case, and gets over the difficulties as it best may, trusting to its good luck to meet the future contingencies by future expedients. At another time it has to retract what it has done. Then it throws the odium upon the ministers, turns them out of office, puts in a new set, and gracefully retraces its steps.

Thus, in the question of the Holy Places, its policy has been vacillating from the beginning, sometimes yielding to one European influence, sometimes to another. SULEIMAN yielded to FRANCIS I. the Protectorate of the Holy Places. The Greeks succeeded in reversing the decree. LOUIS XIV. demanded a restoration. After a period, the Greeks regained possession. While minor contests have been going on from time to time, in which Turkey has always succumbed to the Power that was pressing the hardest at the moment: and when that ceased and the other retaliated, she has abandoned the first, and yielded to the second. Thus, in 1850,—she had first granted to Russia a firman establishing the *status in quo*, that is, she had determined and decreed that the Greeks should remain in possession of the Holy Places which they then held. In 1850, the Marquis de LAVALETTE came, and he came with threatening orders from the Court of the Imperial President, who was then rapidly expanding the form of his despotic power. For a moment, I go from fact to probable conjecture. The Marquis visited Rome on his way, and had an interview with the Pope. LOUIS NAPOLEON had need of the Pope's assistance in some of his designs. He has need of it still. The Marquis de LAVALETTE was instructed (this is my conjecture) to negotiate with the Pope the terms upon which his master should have the countenance of His Holiness in

his political projects. The Pope bargained for the Protectorate of the Holy Places. Here ends conjecture, and facts
again begin. The Marquis *did* come to Constantinople.
He *did* put in a claim for the restoration of the Holy Places
to the Latins. He *did* enforce that claim by certain severe
threats. He *did* assert for France an ancient Protectorate of
the Holy Land. He carried all before him. His violence
and denunciation succeeded in obtaining from the Porte a
firman transferring to the Latins the guardianship of the
most important of the Holy Places. It is here that Russia
first appears upon the field, and she appears as the champion
of the Eastern Church. She interposed her powerful veto.
She insisted upon the execution of the firman previously
granted to her. She, too, threatened; and in the eyes of
Turkey her threats are bigger than those of France. She,
too, succeeded; and the Porte, following its usual policy,
sent secret orders to Syria that the firman granted to
France should not be executed. It was not executed; and
the Marquis de LAVALETTE, who had gone home to report
his victory and to reap his reward, was obliged to hasten
back to Constantinople to re-adjust the disturbed balance,
and to resuscitate his dishonoured firman. This he succeeded in doing, and Russia found herself again baulked by
the Imperial President.

At this point comes in the mission of MENSCHIKOFF.
He was a special envoy on the part of Russia, as LAVALETTE
had been on the part of France. Undoubtedly, his first
instructions were to adjust the question of the guardianship
of the Holy Places. I think there is reason to believe, that at
the first these were his only instructions. At least, if he had
others, they were held in reserve. He came to Constantinople with a great display of power and pride. The Czar
knows well how to deal with the Sultan. The noise of
navies reviewed, and camps visited, of deadly preparations
for war, of armaments gathering in the Crimea, was a
fitting preliminary to the message which he had to bear.
He entered Constantinople as it were in triumph, as the
Ambassador of LOUIS XIV. did, when he came armed with

the same demand. He was escorted by the Greek clergy—
a sufficient indication of the esteem in which the Greek
Church held this mission of MENSCHIKOFF—a sufficient
answer, let me add, to the idle and improbable reports that
the Greeks are unfavourable to the demands of Russia. He
refused to recognize the Reiss Effendi, or Minister for
Foreign Affairs, who, as he alleged, had deceived his master
the Emperor, in the matter of the firmans. He demanded
a full restoration. Here France yielded. LOUIS NAPOLEON
doubtless saw that a contest with Russia would cost more
than the Protectorate of the Holy Places and the friendship
of the Pope would gain for him. He renounced the acts
of his Ambassador, replaced him by a man of milder
qualities, and yielded to the re-establishment of the *status
in quo ante bellum*, the condition of things which prevailed
before this war of diplomatic papers began.

Thus far the mission of MENSCHIKOFF was successful.
He gained that which apparently he came for. But he did
not return. He remained at Constantinople; and the rumour
soon arose that he was pressing other and more important
demands. Amidst the smoke of surmise and doubt and
conjecture, we could not for a time see the truth. At last
it came out, distinctly and in bold relief, that he had asked
of Turkey the Protectorate of the Greek Christians, and
that the Sultan refused thus to sign away his sovereignty.
Now, it is a matter of no importance that I know of, to my
readers, individually and personally, whether MENSCHI-
KOFF made this precise demand or not; and, if he did
make it, whether it was a just demand or not. This, I say,
is of no importance to us personally. But it is of some
importance, if we wish to interest ourselves in the question,
and to learn the truth respecting it, that we should free ourselves from every undue bias; and be prepared to look at the
right in the case steadily and with unjaundiced eye. I think
that the demand of Russia was a just one, and ought to
have been granted; and if my readers will have patience
with me, I will endeavour to make this position as clear to
their minds as it is to my own.

b

We have little information of the grounds upon which Prince MENSCHIKOFF urged his demand. But we do know two things; first, what was the precise character of the demand; and secondly, what was the nature of the stipulation which he required concerning it. He did *not* demand formally that Russia should be acknowledged as the Protector of the Greek Christians, subjects of the Sultan. He *did* demand that Turkey should pledge herself, by convention with Russia, that the ancient immunities and privileges of the Greek Church should be secured to it for all time to come. This was the demand precisely. It did not make Russia in form the Protector of the Greek Church; but it made her so virtually and in reality; since the convention, being made with Russia as a treaty stipulation, she could at all times call for the fulfilment of it, and any violation of the ancient privileges of the Greek Church would be a violation of a compact with Russia. Still, the want of a formal recognition of Russia as Protector, and under that name, is a fact of importance, as I will presently endeavour to show.

Of the second point,—the nature of the contract which Russia required of Turkey,—it is enough to say, that Prince MENSCHIKOFF repeatedly lowered his demand, first, requiring a convention, the highest form of diplomatic contract; next, if I rightly remember (but the point is of no importance), a Vizerial Letter, in which the Grand Vizier becomes the contracting party in behalf of the Sultan; and, finally, a note from the Minister of Foreign Affairs, the lowest form of engagement into which Turkey ever enters. Each of these was an important concession, as each one brought down the solemnity and momentous character of the stipulation to a lower order of engagement; as, for example, the honour of the Empire would be less seriously damaged by a future violation of a compact which stood only in the name of the Minister for Foreign Affairs, than of one, like the first proposed, which bore the royal cypher, and was issued in the name of Majesty. If it be urged that, after all, it is a distinction without a difference, that Russia would compel Turkey, as she certainly would, to abide by her contract, whether it were in the Minister's name or in the Sultan's, it is enough to reply, that Turkey herself places a high estimate of difference upon these different forms of political compact, and that her whole history shows that she has very different senses of obligation respecting them. A note from the Foreign Department is, in fact, one of her most ordinary and approved modes of temporary expedients; and it generally remains in force as long as the minister who gave it remains in office. Having had much experience in observing the courses of Turkish policy, I should say that the note last demanded by Prince MENSCHIKOFF was an utterly useless paper, excepting so far as Russia might have it in her power, from time to time, to enforce the fulfilment of it. The reader will see presently why I have attached so much importance to this matter of form.

I have said that but little is known to us of the grounds upon which Prince MENSCHIKOFF enforced his claims. But the veil of diplomatic secrecy has been raised in one or two places, and gives us an opportunity to catch a glimpse of the workings within. The first argument (which also sets forth the immediate occasion of making the demand), was, that whereas the Porte had deceived Russia repeatedly in the firmans relating to the Holy Places, the Emperor could no longer rely upon so insufficient a guarantee of the rights of the Greek Church, but would require a stipulation by treaty that these rights should not hereafter be invaded. Here comes in the gist of the question. How could Russia demand any such compact from the Sultan with reference to the government of his own subjects? Was it not an arbitrary stretch of power, a violation of international law, an impertinence, and an insult, thus to require a weaker nation to promise that it would rule any portion of its people after a certain rule or mode? It certainly appears so,—it certainly is so, viewing the question as now arising for the first time between Russia and Turkey, and viewing the sovereignty of Turkey as standing till now unimpaired towards all foreign nations. But if it shall appear that that sovereignty, of which so much has been said in a tone as of deep sympathy for the oppressed, be a thing of un-reality, which Turkey does not pretend to sustain towards other Powers, if it be proved that Russia demands no more of her than she has voluntarily granted, and still grants, to others, the question, it seems to me, comes to wear a different aspect, especially if it can be shown that the Russian demand is intended to counterbalance a specific grant made by the Sultan in the opposite direction.

There is no Christian Government, not even our own, which treats Turkey as sovereign and independent. Since the battle of Navarino, she has not only existed by Euro-pean sufferance, but has been governed by European dictation. Each one of the five Great Powers is free to exercise its dictatorship not only in matters affecting its own interests, but in affairs purely Turkish, and in the interior administration of the Government. Hardly a day passes that the Porte does not receive from some one or other of these Powers, in some shape or other, opinions and representations with regard to its conduct, which it dares not neglect; and these opinions and representations oft-times conveyed in language which one friend would hardly venture to use to another. This has especially been true since the compact of 1841, when, after the Syrian war, after the united Powers of Europe had prevented MOHAM-MED ALI from reaching the throne of Turkey, when nought else than their opposition stood in his way, they agreed that the integrity of Turkey should be preserved, and that she should be taken under their united tutelage. From that time to this, Turkey has been under tutors and governors; and a nation under tutors and governors is neither sovereign nor independent. This is a very important view in our present discussion, because it serves to put the conduct of Russia in its true light, whether that light be a more or less amiable one.

I have said that even our own Government does not recognise the sovereignty of Turkey. I will give an illustration of my meaning. I suppose that there is no prerogative of sovereignty more clear and undoubted than the right of a nation to execute its laws over all and on all who reside within its territory. This does not Turkey. No European nation, nor the American Government, allows the Government of Turkey to administer justice to any one of its citizens found in any district in the Ottoman Empire. If an American robs or burns or murders, though it be against one of the Sultan's own subjects, he is not subjected to the execution of the laws of Turkey. He is delivered up to the minister of the United States. Or rather, he is ordinarily allowed to go at large; for the Porte will seldom trouble itself to catch culprits whom it is not at liberty to punish. Hence it arises, that there is probably no capital on the face of the earth where crime is committed with so great impunity as in Constantinople. It is the sewer of Europe, into which the offscourings of the European cities, refugees from justice, blackguards, gamblers and murderers are found in reeking profusion. They rob, they murder, they burn houses, either with perfect impunity, or, at least, beyond the power of the Turkish Government to interfere. Any one who has lived in the Frank quarter of Constantinople, and has felt the necessity of guarding his house against the inroads of thieves whom he cannot punish if he catches them; who knows not but that it may be burnt down over his head, by fellows who can afford to do it for sport or plunder, because they are almost sure to do it with impunity, so difficult is it for a Foreign Minister to adjudicate the case, even if the Turks seize the offender, unless he has from his government, as I believe our Minister now has, a special grant of judicial power; who fears to walk in the street at night unattended, since, in the most public places, he is liable to be robbed without redress; such a one, I say, is little likely to feel any over-degree of respect for a sovereignty which allows these things to pass uncensured, because it has resigned the right of punishing crime in its own dominions, if so be that the crime is committed by a foreigner.

I might illustrate this subject very much at length, and adduce other instances in which our own Government, perhaps almost from necessity, has followed the example of European Governments in not treating Turkey as a sovereign and independent power; while to those Governments it has been, at least for the last twelve years, by its own voluntary concessions, a very vassal and bond-slave. This may not altogether excuse Russia, in her late attempt upon Turkish sovereignty; but it is something for her to be able to shew that she is doing no worse than her neighbours are doing; and it is still more for her to shew that she asks for herself no more than is granted to others. This latter point I will now proceed to prove.

In the year 1844 (subsequent to the European compact of 1841), the Governments of England and France united in a demand upon the Sultan, that he should abrogate the Mohammedan law, which requires that a man apostatising from Mohammedanism shall be put to death. I will not carry you through the long controversy that ensued. It will suffice to say that the Porte evaded, by every device in its power, the execution of the demand. It represented to these great powers that the law in question was a fundamental law of the Empire; that it was a law of their religion, with which the Government could not interfere; that it was based upon a decree of MOHAMMED, whom they believed to be an inspired prophet; that it was, therefore, in their estimation, a revealed law of deity; that if they should attempt to abrogate it, the religious orders would rise in rebellion and incite the common people, over whom they had unbounded sway, to tumult and insurrection. But in vain. England and France were inexorable; and the result was, that on the 21st of March, 1844, the Sultan himself, in his own hand-writing, promised that the law should no more be executed. Compare this now with the present conduct of Russia. She does not ask that any law be abrogated, but only that the *ancient* and *acknowledged* immunities and rights of the Greek Church be secured to it in the future, by a written pledge. She does not ask that the royal word be given. She will be satisfied with a simple note from the Minister for Foreign Affairs. If she is thereby bringing attaint to the sovereignty of Turkey, what have England and France been doing? They are the acknowledged Protectors of all who choose to abandon Islamism. In like manner, and still more recently, England has demanded that the Porte recognise as a separate sect that portion of its subjects who have chosen to leave the Mother Churches of the East and call themselves ' Protestants,' and she has succeeded in the demand. The fact has been proclaimed, with much of congratulation, in this country, and the thanks of the principal Missionary Board in the United States have been rendered to the British Ambassador for his efforts. These are but illustrations, specimens by the way, of the sovereignty of Turkey, as exercised in matters cognate with that which is now in question. They may shew, at least, with how much of grace, England and France can talk of sustaining the independence of the Sultan against the encroachments of his Northern neighbour, and with how much of consistency wise men among ourselves are ready to excite a crusade, with the cross reversed, for the support of the Great Mohammedan Power of the East.

But we have not yet reached the true strength of Russia's argument. I will introduce it by an illustration. In the year 1841, I was the guest, for a few weeks, of the Syrian Patriarch, in his Monastery, in the confines of Mesopotamia. He treated me with great courtesy, and commended to my attention a question which had arisen between him and a sect of seceders, who had left his Church and joined the Romish communion. A large amount of valuable Church property near Damascus had been seized by them, and he had commenced a suit at the Porte for the purpose of recovering possession of it. The property was an endowment of the Syrian Church, and the titles by which it was held were as clear and as strong as any titles to property can be imagined to be. The seceders had got possession of it, and were using it for their own purposes, and especially for the purpose of extending their own sect in Syria. I promised him such assistance as I might be able to render at Constantinople; and, on my return, I took the matter in hand. There was then there a Syrian Bishop, who represented the Patriarch in the controversy, and urged the claims of the Syrian Church before the Porte. The question lingered in a manner altogether unexpected. The Porte acknowledged the justice of the Syrian cause. The documents laid before it were too clear to admit a reasonable doubt. But still it hesitated to accord justice. We were convinced that some hostile influence was in operation. Upon inquiry, it was found that the French Ambassador was opposed to a settlement, and was using his influence at the Porte to prevent it. I advised the Bishop to protest against this interference of a foreign power, in a question which concerned only two parties of the Sultan's subjects. He did so, and the reply was, that France was the acknowledged Protector of the Eastern Christians who owned spiritual allegiance to the Pope, or, as the French Ambassador was pleased to express it, " the hereditary Protector of the Oriental Catholics." In this character, he had interfered in behalf of the Papal seceders from the Syrian Church. In this character he was acknowledged by the Porte through the whole of a controversy which lasted nearly two years. And in this character he finally succeeded, against the plainest dictates of justice and equity, in intimidating the Porte so far as to prevent it from restoring the property. It is still in the hands of the Syrian Papists, and is likely, unless Russia succeeds in her present demand to remain there for ever.

I was at the time impressed with the conviction, that this Protectorate of France had no foundation in any *formal* concession made by the Porte, but that it had grown up unawares and by degrees from the old habit the Catholic Majesties of France had had of interfering in behalf of Oriental Papists. I had known that it was a pretence of long standing, that the Latin missions in the East had found shelter under the protection of it, and that it had now come to be practically and fully acknowledged by the Porte. It was an established and undisputed Protectorate. The British Ambassador, with whom I conferred upon the subject, and who aided the Syrians in their suit, but without any of the advantage which his French colleague derived from the right of protection, was of the same opinion with myself, that France could show no *documentary* basis for such a claim. The plea was, therefore, put in, at one period of the suit, that France was exercising this Protectorate without any just title. But, on the one hand, the Porte was not at all disposed to listen to the plea, because France certainly had what is a final and unanswerable argument with an Oriental, the argument of custom,—she had always been doing it, and that was enough,—and, on the other, the French Ambassador did deign to send to the Porte some document in which such a grant was made. The poor Bishop, when he came home, thoroughly disheartened, from this interview, told me that the document presented was some 150 years old, but he could not understand the exact tenor of it. I afterwards discovered its meaning. It was, I presume, a copy of the treaty, or code of capitulations, granted by the Sultan to Louis XIV. of France, in 1673, in which I find these several concessions, first, ' that the King of France be recognised the sole Protector of the Catholics,' (that is, of the Oriental Romanists, subjects of the Sultan,) ' in the East;' secondly, ' that Churches be erected or repaired [by them] without the previous authorisation of the Porte;' and thirdly, ' that the Holy Shrines shall be restored to the possession of the Latins, because they were conquered by Frenchmen in the Crusades.'

Here we have, at full length, an acknowledged Protectorate of the Latin schismatics in the East, a Protectorate *tot verbis;* a change in the fundamental law of the Empire and of Mohammedanism which forbids the increase of Christian Churches; this law abrogated in behalf of the Papal seceders from the Oriental Communions, while it remained, and has ever since remained, and, unless Russia succeeds in her present demand, is likely to remain, so long as the Turkish Empire stands, in full force against those

communions themselves; and, finally, the possession of the
Holy Places, the undoubted patrimony of the Greek Church,
which, if it were seized by Frenchmen at the Crusades,
was afterwards lost by them. These stipulations were em-
bodied, with others hardly less important, but not bearing
so directly upon the question now before us, in a convention
of the highest character, as grants from the Sultan himself to
the King of France. These stipulations have never since been
annulled. They are still in force; and it is under them
that France is acting at this day as the acknowledged Protector of the Oriental Roman Catholics, representing their
interests freely and constantly at the Porte, and extending,
by the whole weight of her powerful influence, the domain
of Popery in the East.

Notwithstanding the last of these important concessions,
the Greeks, about the middle of the last century, re-obtained
possession of the Holy Places, and have held them, with
various struggles, until this time.   When, in 1850, France
re-advanced her claim, doubtless in concert with the Pope,
and to gain, as I have supposed, the favour which LOUIS
NAPOLEON needed from him, that claim was put forward
distinctly in her character as Protector of the Eastern
Romanists; and when it was finally withdrawn, on account
of the threatening attitude of Russia, at a moment when
the newly created Emperor of France could ill afford to
lose the friendship of the European Monarchies, it was
declared by France, in express terms, that, ' while she was
entitled by capitulations to a supremacy-in the Churches of
the Shrines of the Holy Land, she would not, from a spirit
of moderation, adhere, for the present, to the letter of these
instruments;' thus making her concession one of grace, and
not of duty.

We now begin to see the real foundation of the difference
between Russia and Turkey, and the true nature of the
question at issue.   Russia has been acknowledged, for more
than a century, as the nearest friend of the Greek Church.
She has been empowered, by treaties with Turkey, one of
which, that of Kainarji, bears date 1774, to represent the

interests of the Greek Church to the Porte, and to appear
n defence of its rights; that is, she has been allowed *to
make representations to the Porte of whatever she thought
might concern the welfare of the Greek Church*, and the
Porte promised by that treaty, to lend a friendly ear to her
representations. This is the whole extent of the concession hitherto made to *her.* Under this concession, she has
always,—at least since my own acquaintance with Turkey
began, she has always been forward to do all in her power
to defend the interests of the Greek Church, to represent
them to the Porte, and to urge them upon the Sultan's
attention. She has done this informally, as the nature of
her contract with Turkey allowed, as a friend of the Greek
Church, and as an ally of the Sultan. But she has never
assumed, as she had no acknowledged right to assume, the
character of. 'Protector of the Greek Church.' That title
has never been accorded to her by the Porte; and when
her representations have succeeded, it has been by the
influence which, at the moment, she happened to have with
the Ottoman Government. Her stipulated right has been
no more than has been, and is constantly, fully exercised
by other Governments, (and, among others, by our own
Government,) which have not the same terms of treaty with
Turkey. England, Austria, Prussia, and the United States,
all within my own knowledge, some of them many times
within my own knowledge, have used the same privilege.
Their representatives at the Porte have advised the Turkish
Government with regard to the religious interests of some
portion or other of the Sultan's subjects. The only difference is, that Russia has done it systematically and constantly
in behalf of the Greek Church, with an eye ever open to
its welfare, and under the sanction of a treaty. England,
Austria, Prussia, and the United States have done it occa-
sionally and without treaty, yet in practice quite as fully as
Russia herself. Her only advantage has been that she had
an acknowledged right to make representations, and they
had none; but in reality the time has long gone by when
any respectable Power stood in such awe of Turkey, or had

such respect for her sovereignty, that it would hesitate to
advise her on any subject of her internal Government on
which it might please to proffer an opinion. One does it,
and all do it; the frequency varying according to the occasions which they may severally have; while Turkey bears
it with the exemplary patience of a Nation that cannot help
itself, thanks them for their advice, makes fair promises of
following it, and shirks them, when they are distasteful, in
the best way that she can.

It has been said, and much importance has been attached
to the alleged fact, that the Greeks themselves are opposed
to this intervention of Russia in their behalf. We hear
it reported, that the Greek Patriarch and other Greek
Bishops have requested the honour of accompanying the
Sultan to the camp in the spring. The present Greek
Patriarch, ANTHIMOS, has held the office before, and I
presume he is the same with whom, during that incum-
bency, it was my lot to form an intimate acquaintance. If
so, he is a venerable, aged man, of easy temper, of mild
manners, of inoffensive conversation. He is such a man as
the Porte uniformly puts into the Patriarchate when it
wishes a man to its mind: for, although the Greek Patriarch
is elected by the Metropolitical Synod, its action is subject
to the dictation of the Government, when the Government
chooses to express an opinion on the subject; and its opinion,
I hardly need say, is never disregarded. In the present
instance, the Patriarch was put in evidently for the present emergency. He will yield to every request of the
Sultan, he will issue documents declaring his aversion to
the Russian Protectorate, he will accompany His Majesty
to the camp; but, through all, he and every member of the
Greek Church will see, and know, that their only hope of
rescue from the domination of Mohammedanism (which
they hate universally with the intense hatred that a thousand years of wrongs have accumulated), lies in the ad-
vancing power of Russia. I have not a doubt that the
Patriarch ANTHIMOS, if it be he whom I have formerly
seen exercising his office in full understanding with the

Russian Ambassador at Constantinople, preserves an under-standing with Russia still; and that though he may seem, from the necessity of the case, as he believes, to keep on good terms with the Porte, lest his people suffer from some outbreak of Mohammedan bigotry; though he may issue letters in the interest of the Sultan, which he regards as mere involuntary acts of office dictated by his Turkish masters; and though he may proceed with His Majesty to the field of battle, of his own accord, as the newspapers say, yet of an accord preceded by a private intimation from the Porte which he dare not disregard;—notwithstanding all this, he and his whole Church are as much friends of Russia as they were a few years ago; they feel their dependence upon her as much now as they did then; and they know that if Russia fails in this contest, the failure is their own, the Oriental Church will be left without protection to the mercies of the Mohammedan, the tenderest of which are cruel. The contest began in rescuing their rights, which had been violated in the matter of the Holy Places. This was a great, an inestimable favour to them. The present demand is that those and all other ancient rights of the Greek Church be secured by written compact; and to suppose, for a moment, that the Greek Patriarch and his co-religionists are opposed to an agency that proposes to accomplish this for them; an agency which has given them all the protection which they have had the last fifty years, and which gives them all that they can hope for in the time to come; that they are willing, nay, desirous, to see Russia defeated in a matter which is life and death to them, a matter in which defeat would leave them without a single remaining safeguard against the encroachments of the Church of Rome, sustained, as she is, in the East, by the Protectorate of one of the most powerful governments of Europe; is, one would think, too great an absurdity even to be transmitted by telegraph.

To return. The true question at issue is purely a Christian question; and by this aspect of it our sympathies respecting it should be mainly regulated. However, as men,

we might be conscious of a certain kindliness of feeling
towards the Nation which is the weaker in the contest;
however natural and spontaneous this feeling may be, yet,
as Christians and Churchmen, we cannot avoid, if we would
view it aright, the entrance of a higher principle into the
consideration. It is really a question between the Oriental
and the Latin Church. Divested of all collateral issues, it
is simply a question whether Eastern Christianity shall have
the same kind and degree of foreign protection that is accorded to the comparatively insignificant body of those who,
remaining as before subjects of the Sultan, have seceded, or
are the descendants of those who have seceded, from the
Oriental Church to the Papal Communion. I fearlessly
avow, that I do represent the true American and Protestant
feeling and principle, when I say, that equal political advantages and guarantees should be granted to the two hostile
Communions. If either is to have a privilege above the other,
it should be in favour of the old established Christianity of
the country. But even this is not asked. The demand is
simply that the Greek Church be placed upon the same
footing with the Papal Schism. France is the acknowledged
Protector of the latter. Russia demands a similar guarantee
for the former. Nay, though nearer to the Greek Church
than France can pretend to be to the Latin, her demand is
less than that which has been accorded to France. She
does not ask to be recognised as Protector of the Greek
Church, which France is acknowledged to be to the Latin
sect. This is a title that covers a right to interfere, in any
manner or degree, and on any subject that may have a
bearing, however remote, upon the real or pretended welfare
of the Papal Communion. She asks only that *the ancient
and acknowledged rights of the Greek Church be secured by
written guarantee.* She does not ask that this writing be in
the highest form of diplomatic contract, as has been granted
to France; but is willing that it be of the lowest and least
formal kind that is known in international negotiation. She
asks the very least that can be supposed sufficient to secure
the Greek Church against the encroachments of its great

enemy. Is there any injustice in all this? I confess that I cannot see it. My every feeling of truth and equity convinces me that the claim of Russia is just and moderate, and that it ought to be sustained. The Four Powers have virtually acknowledged as much in their Vienna Note, which accorded to Russia substantially what she had desired. How can they or any of them, go to war with her upon any possible pretext, unless it be that they cannot afford to see her extend her conquests in Turkey by the acquisition of territory? This, if there be a European war, will be the only ground of it. But it presents an issue entirely aside from the right and wrong of the question in debate between Russia and Turkey. And it is well worth while to remember, in case such a war should break out, (which may GOD, in His mercy to the Nations, forefend!) that upon the real point in dispute, the enemies of Russia in that war have acknowledged the rectitude of her cause, in the Note which they recommended to the Porte to adopt, and with which Russia declared herself satisfied, as answering sufficiently her demands.

But it is impossible not to foresee, that a European war will, in its results, greatly affect the question upon which I have now treated. It is impossible, I suppose, that such a war should not leave Russia crippled and defeated; for, however successful she might be when opposed singly to so weak an antagonist as Turkey, there is no chance, humanly speaking, of her competing with the navy of England and the legions of France. She will be defeated; and what thus becomes of the real questions at issue? Turkey declares that even her former treaty with Russia, conferring, as it did, very imperfect advantages upon her as the friend of the Greek Church at the Porte, is annulled by the war. To what, then, are the Eastern Christians left? On the one hand, to the powerful enmity of France, waging a religious war upon them through the ever-active agency of the Church of Rome, and, on the other, to the uncovenanted mercies of the Mohammedan. What a dire prospect does this present for the ancient Christianity of the East!

What a dire prospect for the cause of the Anglican Church in that quarter, which is, I believe, the cause of the purest Catholicity!* What a dire prospect for our common Protestantism! What a dire prospect for our whole Christianity, excepting for the Church of Rome, which will alone gain by a European war! And if there is a thought which comes over the mind, as we contemplate this possible future, with a more melancholy interest than any other, it is the thought that our dear mother-land, Old England, the Bulwark of Protestantism, will be found fighting the battles of Rome. For France it is consistent, it is to be expected. But for England! alas, alas! if the Cross of St. George is to be borne over the waters of the Mediterranean, not alone to carry aid and comfort to the powers of darkness which rally under the banner of the Crescent, but to inflict a wound upon the ancient Christianity of the East, from which it may never recover! Alas, alas! if in the judgment that shall come upon the nations, it be found that England, with the faith that she has purified through fire and blood, with the memory of martyrs clustering like a crown of glory round her head, with her primitive and Apostolic Church, derived from the pure fountain of the East, when that fountain sent abroad its clearest and most refreshing waters over other lands, England, Protestant England, the truest friend of the Reformation, shall have borne a part, and that the principal part, in sending back upon the East the curse from which she is so happily delivered, in aiding the most aggressive Church on earth in propagating, unopposed, and with every vantage for success, the corrupt faith and worship which neither our fathers nor we were able to bear!

* It is a matter well worthy of note, that England, by taking side with the party that represents the Latin interests in this strife, incurs for herself, and, by necessary consequence, for the English Communion, the deep and probably perpetual hostility of the Greek Church. Indeed, every religious consideration seems to be merged in her political jealousy of Russia.

SOME

OBSERVATIONS

ON THE

WAR IN THE CRIMEA.

EXTRACT FROM THE DUKE OF WELLINGTON'S INSTRUCTIONS
TO LIEUT.-COL. FLETCHER, R.E.

Lisbon, 28th Oct., 1809.

" He will examine and report upon the means of making a good road of *communication* from the plain across the hills into the valley of Cadafoes, and calculate the time and labour it will take.

" He will intrench a post at Torres Vedras for 5,000 men. He will examine the road from Torres Vedras to Cabaca de Montoechique; and fix upon the spots at which to break it up, as might stop or delay the enemy, &c."

LONDON:
SIMPKIN, MARSHALL, AND CO.;
AND
CHELTENHAM: HENRY DAVIES, MONTPELLIER LIBRARY:
1855.

THE WAR IN THE CRIMEA.

A RETROSPECT of the few last months may be so
far useful, as to shew that those who, from their rank
and influence, have it in their power to fill situations
of great responsibility, should well consider what they
undertake, and that from them some little knowledge
of the circumstance of war might be expected. Are
the destinies, the lives, the honor of thousands of
brave men to be hazarded? Is the happiness of so
many English firesides to be confided to inexperience
and ignorance? How many hearts might now be
beating, cheered by the prospect of honor, and a return to the welcome and admiration of relatives and
friends, who mourn over losses that can never be
repaired. Alas! alas! that the lost time of the few
last months could be recalled, the precious hours
wasted at Malta, at Stamboul, at Varna—where,
extenuated by disease, disappointed by inglorious

inaction, our noble army lay fretting in idleness, depressed in spirit, and humiliated at the recital of the gallant efforts on the banks of the Danube.

Well may Sir William Napier be indignant at the assertion that there exists but one officer who could be consulted by the ducal war minister. Why there was hardly a veteran at any of the clubs who did not express his surprise at the incomprehensible apathy of the Government. It was manifest to all that the Autocrat, under the mask of religion, projected a division of the spoils of the sick man; that he calculated on old and long continued friendship, and the feelings of a gentleman, to support his devastations. Did he not insult England by the offer of a bribe, and treat with contempt the empire of Austria? We are told, from high authority, that our temporising conduct saved the Turkish capital. Could it be believed that garrulous vapourings of peace arrested for an instant the march of the Autocrat to the goal from whence he was to view the Golden Horn, and the waters of the Bosphorus, as a master? The grasping views of the Autocrat were well known, and the unprincipled policy of his empire a matter of history.

Why, it was asked, did we not tell the Muscovite that, when he crossed the Pruth, we should occupy the Turkish territory, secure Constantinople, sweep the Euxine and the Baltic, reduce his towns and his fortresses to ashes, destroy his commerce, and teach him that a free people knew how to curb the atrocious will of a despot. This we could have said—and more, this we could have done. But what did we do?—we allowed our noble fleet ingloriously to be anchored in the Bosphorus, whilst our Turkish allies were cruelly butchered and destroyed at Sinope. We spared the granaries from which the Autocrat feeds his armies. We allowed the principalities, gloriously regained by Turkish valour, to be occupied by the cautious and cunning Austrian, who paralysed, at the most vital moment, the conquering Mussulman. It will be only after the first serious conflict with the Muscovite that Austrian sincerity and co-operation may be relied on.

True it is that an army, such as never quitted the shores of England, had been collected, with every quality that troops should have. So far, the Government deserves credit. But what is that army now, from want of due administration? The Duke of

Wellington, whose capacious mind embraced every great, as well as every minor duty, thought it prudent to appoint a general officer at Lisbon, to arrange all matters relating to reinforcements, embarkation, hospitals, &c., and this duty was well done. Why was not such an appointment made at Constantinople? The *Times*, of the 2nd inst., says :—" What are we to think of a system, under which the purveyor satisfies his ideas of official duty by piling up medical stores and comforts of all kinds, and refusing to give them out, even when, for months together, there is an urgent demand for them." Good God! can any common language express the feelings of disgust that a miserable official should have it in his power so to deprive the sick and wounded?—to withhold from those who were suffering, as none had suffered before, and who had fought and conquered with a heroism unparalleled in all history.

From ignorance, and want of attention to a proper arrangement, the medical department has been defective in every point, notwithstanding the unwearied and meritorious exertions of the medical officers in the field, in the hospitals, and on board of crowded, unprovided, and infectious transports.

Even the vicissitudes of the seasons were forgotten. Shelter from the cold and the wet was neglected—warm and suitable clothing unprovided—no comforts sent direct from Government—and no encouragement given to suttlers to supply articles of grocery, cooking utensils, &c., so indispensably necessary to officers and men—raw coffee issued. Why was not all this done, instead of permitting the hard-worked officer and soldier to depend on foreigners at unheard-of ruinous prices. General Canrobert says—" Thanks to the wise *foresight* of the Emperor and his *Government*, the army enjoys relative comforts which make it gaily support the fatigues it has to undergo." Surely, medicines, comforts, beds, &c., could have been sent to the respective hospital stations, consigned to the senior medical officers, and distributed by them, freed from all dilatory forms. Instructions sent to disembark, without delay, stores injudiciously stowed on board of the *Prince* of medicines and clothing for 40,000 men, so much needed by our ragged soldiers, instead of placing her in a position to be dashed to pieces on the Crimean rocks, and her inestimable cargo to be lost. No suitable vessels were fitted up as hospitals. The invalided soldiers sent home in ships with nothing but the hard and naked boards to lie on. Does the Duke of Newcastle mean to say that no officer but one could have told him to take these ordinary precautions? The Emperor of the French and his War Minister were not above thinking of the comforts of their men. Equal we may be to our brave allies in the shock of battle, but they are our masters in all else. Had reinforcements been sent after the battle of the Alma commensurate with the power of England, roads might have been made and strong defences constructed to render our position like that of Torres Vedras—impregnable. There would then have been no difficulty in the transport of guns, stores, and provisions, and our soldiers need not have been deprived of half their rations.

As yet, nothing has been done but to secure a footing in the Crimea. We have now to conquer two hundred thousand Russian savages, only formidable to the helpless wounded : to attack in front, flank, and rear, and to gain victories with great results. Then we may enter Sebastopol as conquerors, and, I was going to say, not till then ;

but the heroism of the conquerers of the Alma,
Balaklava, and Inkerman is beyond calculation.
His Grace of Newcastle may undervalue the
opinions of the remaining veterans of the Peninsula.
He is welcome to say that every officer is in the
Crimea, save one, from whom he could receive
advice ; but there are still officers in England
"with sagacity enough to see through his incapacity," to lament over the stout hearts that
struggle against unheard-of ills, with the fortitude
of heroes and the resignation of Christians. With
bitter regret it is to be hoped our rulers will look
back to the neglect of the three last months, that
in their dreams they will picture to themselves the
worn-out hero, the shade of what he was, the
cholera-stricken soldier, the shivering, drenched
sentinel, issuing from the trenches knee-deep in
mud, without the prospect of shelter or the consolation of decent cleanliness, the officers without
baggage, the men without necessaries. Willingly
would the ministers throw the burden on other
shoulders, but as the gallant and distinguished
historian of the Peninsula says, "let them slink
away while the universal shout arises of 'God and
our right.'"

The people of England are not to be deceived by Parliamentary orations, in which an attempt is made to prove that all has been done officially right, knowing, as we all do, that everything has gone practically wrong. Great as the merit may be in the formation of such an expedition, it is equally important that the utmost care be taken in directing the various materials of which it is composed, to their respective destinations, in a wise arrangement of all the details, and in facilitating and simplifying their distribution. The capacity to do this must be the result of experience. He who takes upon himself such an administration, should know what a soldier wants; that he requires to be sheltered from the storm, to rest after his harassing duties, and to care, consolation, and comfort when he is sick or wounded; that means be at hand to bear him from the field of battle, and, if to be embarked. ships fitted up as hospitals with every convenience. Read the letters from the educated officer, the simple-hearted soldier, from the father, the son, the husband, and the friend, and say whether such should be the victims of aristocratic incapacity. Nothing can be more touching than the expression of a high sense of feeling for the honor of their

Queen and Country, of patience under unequalled sufferings, and of determination to persevere to the last in the execution of their duty.

A marked tenderness has been shewn to the home authorities—not so towards the military commanders. It remains to be known whether Lord Raglan represented his wants after the Alma; if not, he is to blame. But the War Minister should have known, without such representation, that the diminished state of the troops, by battle and disease, required a strong reinforcement. Was it to be expected that our over-worked, ragged, bare-footed soldiers could capture a place strengthened by every resource of a great empire? But we have been doing, by our driblets of reinforcements, what the great Duke said England should not do, "making a little war."

I say it was impossible for Lord Raglan or his departments, with the means at their disposal, to fortify his position, to make roads, &c., &c., and, at the same time, to carry on the siege. I deny that the incompetency of the staff of the British army is notorious; such an assertion more aptly applies to her Majesty's Government. I repeat that the *great, great* error was, in not sending out an effectual reinforcement to the army immediately after the Alma, and that ministers should have done, many months ago, what they are now doing at the eleventh hour.

England expected Sebastopol to fall after the occupation of Balaklava; and every nerve, of both soldier and sailor, was stretched to the utmost to do this. Sir De Lacy Evans, in his farewell letter to Lord Raglan, says :—" The various exigencies to be provided for in other points, at that time, scarcely left it *possible*, I believe, to afford any material re-inforcement or means for the construction of defences." If such an important point of the position could not be strengthened from want of men, surely nothing could be spared to make roads, or to make those necessary works required in the harbour of Balaklava.* The French did all this, because their men were in the trenches only once in five nights, and not harassed, as our debilitated and ragged soldiers, by constant duty. Lord Raglan has been twitted for not sufficiently showing himself to

* As far as the army is concerned.

his army. What benefit could result from the old and disabled soldier destroying his remaining energy and health by unnecessary exposure to evils he had no power to remedy?—At the post of danger, and where the battle raged, there he was to be found.

Let us cease sending driblets of men to perish the instant they land. Expose not the unseasoned soldier to all the vicissitudes of cold and wet, of hunger, of night after night in the trenches, to be struck down by disease till he languishes and dies. I say, let us cease to do this, but send a force of thirty—aye, fifty thousand men worthy of England, and let them at once attack the Russian in all the freshness of their strength and valour. Mr. H. G. Osborne, in his letter in the *Times* of the 2nd inst., says, " our army must be strengthened at *once* in numbers—strengthened in every detail which can make it efficient."

Much has been said of the organization of our staff, as if the fault of our present unfortunate position, lay with them. It may be true that undue favour has been shown to the aristocracy, but I do not admit the justice of the severe remarks made on them. The scions of our noble blood have not been wanting in their duty ; nor do I think that the education at Sandhurst, useful as that may be, is absolutely required to form a staff officer. I have known some of the worst and most negligent regimental officers come from thence. It is the spirit, the energy, the intelligence, and the enthusiasm of the soldier, that is inherent and born with the man that makes the officer; the eye that can see, the head that can think, and the heart that can execute ; the moral courage that fears no responsibility. What requires more resolution and intelligence than a cavalry officer who has to seize the moment of a charge, that exists but for a moment, and which decides the combat? Let us recall Marengo, and the heroes brought forth by the French revolution.

If ever a people, on their bended knees, should implore the protection of Him that rules the battle and quells the storm ; if ever mothers should teach their infants to lisp orisons to the most high, it is at this time, when dire misfortune impends over a nation, and bodes the destruction of her bravest sons.

H. DAVIES, MONTPELLIER LIBRARY, CHELTENHAM.

THE

SOLDIER

THAT WENT NOT TO

SEBASTOPOL.

"A man should never be ashamed to own he has been in the wrong,
which is but saying, in other words, that he is wiser
to-day than he was yesterday."—POPE.

SECOND EDITION.

LONDON:

LUMLEY, 126, HIGH HOLBORN;

WARD AND CO., 27, PATERNOSTER ROW.

AND ALL BOOKSELLERS.

M.DCCC.LV.

THE AUTHOR

DEDICATES THIS EDITION

TO

HIS BRETHREN OF THE CHURCH OF ENGLAND—

THE FOLLOWERS OF THE PRINCE OF PEACE

BY BAPTISM AND VOWS:

TO

ALL WILLING TO HEAR BOTH SIDES OF THE QUESTION;

AND

TO PARENTS ESPECIALLY

ABOUT TO CHOOSE FOR THEIR SONS THE PROFESSION

OF ARMS:—

AND BEGS TO SUBSCRIBE HIMSELF

THEIR VERY FAITHFUL FRIEND AND SERVANT,

𝔄 𝔓𝔯𝔢𝔰𝔟𝔶𝔱𝔢𝔯 𝔬𝔣 𝔱𝔥𝔢 ℭ𝔥𝔲𝔯𝔠𝔥 𝔬𝔣 𝔈𝔫𝔤𝔩𝔞𝔫𝔡.

ADVERTISEMENT TO THE SECOND EDITION.

In issuing a second edition of this pamphlet, the Author begs to notice an objection or two urged to the former edition. First, that the title implied, that soldiers and Christians were essentially opposite characters. Now, whatever views the Author himself may entertain on this subject, he has no desire to wound the feelings of those who may happen to have friends in the service of their country, and whose sympathies would naturally be enlisted on that side. All he desires is, that his readers may be induced to look at the question of war from a religious point of view; and, with this object, he has altered the *Title*, in the hope of removing any prejudice that may thereby be excited against the subject itself.

Another objection urged is, that the arguments of the soldier are *purposely* weaker than those of the Christian. This, as a matter of fact, is not correct; since the discussion contained in the following pages is not a mere fiction, but one which actually took place at ———, in the county of ———, in the month of June last. Five clergymen—advocates of the present war — were asked to show what proofs, passages, or arguments, could be adduced from Christianity to justify a *Christian* in engaging in war at all. They stated as their conviction, that the arguments here put into the mouth of the soldier, were all that could be properly adduced from the New Testament; and they stated, also, that these were amply sufficient to justify our part in the tragedy now being enacted at Sebastopol.

Moreover, if the reader will take the trouble to look at the various pro-war sermons that have lately been published, he will find that, with an unimportant exception, they advance nothing more than the soldier has here said. The writer has in one instance—the exception referred to—met with an argument, if such it can be called, which the soldier has not brought forward. In a sermon on " the *lawfulness!* of war", the text "He that hath no sword, let him sell his garment and buy one"—St. Luke xxii, 36, is actually quoted to prove that our mission to the East is of Christian authority. Surely a little reflection would have shown the preacher that, if the ' Prince of Peace' had intended to arm His followers, He would not have said " *It is enough*", when told they had but two swords among them; since two swords could not have gone far to arm twelve persons. The misapplication of the text therefore is palpable.

It is not surprising, then, to find the same preacher adducing also the instances of the " good centurion, whose servant Jesus restored to health, and Cornelius the man of prayer and almsdeeds." But he neither attempts to *prove* (and the *onus probandi* lies with him who makes the assertion) that Cornelius so belied the lives and practice of the early converts as to dye his hands in blood after becoming a Christian; nor that the " good centurion" was any more of a Christian than the Syrophenician woman, or the man at Gadara, or any other of the afflicted subjects of our Lord's miracles.

Such, however, are the arguments which are supposed to justify Christians in invoking the benedictions of the Prince of Peace upon the swords, rockets, bombshells, and bayonets, now at Sebastopol. The great question is, are these arguments conclusive? Do they—can they—carry conviction to unprejudiced, truth-seeking minds? It behoves us to weigh the matter well; for even the *Times* admits that, "*if there is any subject in the whole sphere of human action, on which there ought to be no doubt or demur, it is the awful business of war... Almost any question, indeed, of mere secular import may be left open for the variety and fallibility of human judgment: but in war, we are assuming, as we needs must assume, the tremendous prerogative of Heaven—the assertion of justice by the sword. The men who takes the responsibility of sending fleets and armies to kill, to burn, to waste and destroy;—to spread ruin among millions, to sow the seeds of endless resentments, to stop the progress of civilization, and drive the human race back again to the desert, ought to be very certain, very hearty, in his hideous work.*"*

August 1st, 1855.

* *Times'* Leading Article, July 14, 1855.

PART I.

———

"Whoever is afraid of submitting any question, civil or religious, to the test of free discussion, seems to me to be more in love with his own opinions than with truth."—BISHOP WATSON.

SOLDIER. I am going to the Crimea on Sunday next, in the Steamer *Mars*. Will you give me your prayers?

CHRISTIAN. Give you my *prayers!* Yes, verily, if you can show me that you ought to have them.

SOL. Why, a Christian ought to be always ready to pray for a fellow Christian.

CHRISTN. That depends upon the object for which the prayer is asked; but, is it that that you are going to do at the Crimea?

SOL. No, I am going to fight, and I ask you to pray for success upon our arms. I think, moreover, it is the least you can do, seeing that we are endeavouring to protect you from oppression and injustice, and to leave you in the quiet enjoyment of your family and property, beneath the sheltering ægis of our free institutions and the *prestige* of our mighty name.

CHRISTN. Would you go if you were not *paid* for it?

Sol. On your own principle, the labourer is worthy of his hire. My payment is therefore a matter of right.

Christn. That is not the question; the question is, whether you would go if there were no promotion, no honours, no pay annexed to the expedition. Would you go and expose your life, simply that I might enjoy our free institutions and drive about in my carriage?

Sol. I cannot say that I would. But I have chosen the profession of a soldier, and in that profession I hope to rise. I naturally expect, therefore, to be rewarded for my labour, just as you do in your profession.

Christn. Very well; then don't say you are going to hazard your life to "protect" me, &c. That may be the result of your going, but it is not the *motive* which impels you. What moves you individually is *pay*; or, which is the same thing, some personal advantage—stars, ribbons, fame, &c. Something which will accrue to yourself, apart from any benefit others may derive from the expedition.

Sol. Undoubtedly. Such is my reason for exchanging into the regiment now going to Sebastopol.

Christn. This point then is disposed of. You are not going there in that pure philanthropic spirit which you would have me believe just now; nor are you going out of *love* to anybody; nor to pray for anybody; but you pack up revolvers and bullets, and sharpen your sword, just as a butcher does when he goes to the slaughter-house, and you set out determined to kill your brother, or lop off his arm, or gouge out his eye, or lacerate his body if he resist you ;—less merciful than the butcher, who never treats his victims thus—and all because it is your *profession* to kill ; and for the exercise of this profession you are to be paid. Now, don't you think it would be more in accordance with the principles of Christianity, if you were to choose a profession a little more exalted and humane ?*

SOL. But what would become of us as a nation if we had no soldiers ?

CHRISTN. Why, we should become more Christian and not need them. Every element of evil must go on re-producing itself in some form or other. If then, war be an evil, we shall not suppress it by increasing its elements; and consequently shall become less Christian, as we become more warlike. But where did you learn that Christianity recognizes any such thing as national distinctions ? If you are to see a brother-soul in every human being, and are required to " do good unto all men" because of such relationship, the idea of " Patriotism" explodes at once.

---

* " That men should kill one another for want of somewhat else to do (*which is the case of all volunteers in war*), seems to be so horrible to humanity, that there needs no divinity to control it."—CLARENDON.

SOL. Do you mean to say that the profession of a soldier is therefore un-Christian? However you may regard it as inhuman, I have yet to learn that it is un-Christian; and it was upon this ground, that your surprise at my asking you to pray for success upon our arms, astonished me. The Russians, as the enemy of your country, are as much your enemies as mine.

CHRISTN. Yes; quite as much, and Christianity teaches me not to kill my enemies, but to love them and pray for them.

SOL. Where does it teach you that you are not to kill your enemies?

CHRISTN. In the New Testament.

SOL. But people were commanded to kill in the Old Testament.

CHRISTN. That was under a very different dispensation—a dispensation of temporal rewards and punishments. We live under a dispensation whose kingdom is not of this world, and whose rewards and punishments are not meted out here, but hereafter. The Jews were commanded to take up arms, certainly, *but never for pay;* and, so far as I know, only against the enemies of God, for sins of idolatry, immorality, &c. And, if God gives me a similar command, I am ready to do the same; but not till then.

SOL. Then you mean to say, that there is in the New Testament, the dispensation under which we live—that which forbids a man to be a soldier? I should like very much to know what it is.

CHRISTN. I do mean to say so; and you shall be the judge. What is the New Testament from beginning to end, but one universal principle of Peace? What the Author of Christianity, but the Prince of Peace? Is not this the name which He chose for Himself? And did not the Spirit prophesy that, under His dispensation "Nation was no longer to lift up sword against nation, nor to learn war any more;—that swords were to be beaten into plough-shares and spears into pruning hooks."—Is. ii.—4. Micah iv.—3; and that universal peace and love were to be the essential characteristics of His reign. Now are peace and love the essential characteristics of the profession of a soldier?

SOL. This time has not yet arrived; and, until it does arrive, we must take things as we find them.

CHRISTN. What a fatalist! 'The time not arrived!' No, nor ever will arrive, so long as Christians consent to become soldiers. Your profession does more than any other to prevent the arrival of this happy period.

SOL. I suppose you are one of the Peace Society, —a set of fanatics, who sent out three of their number to convert the Emperor of Russia at the beginning of this struggle; and well they got laughed at for their pains—or, I should rather say, their folly. Besides, what good did they do?

A 3

CHRISTN. They did this much good : they showed the Emperor that Christian feeling was not quite extinct in England if it was in Russia; that there were at least some here, who recognized the principle of not rendering evil for evil. But when you speak of ' Fanatics,' you must remember that the Apostles and first Preachers of Christianity were called " Fanatics" for preaching these very doctrines of " Peace on earth; good will towards men." If you call them members of the Peace Society, you may call me the same if you please; we certainly do belong to such an institution, now something more than 1800 years old.

SOL. But if Christianity be opposed to war, how comes it that the Apostles took so many of their illustrations from the life and calling of a soldier? Surely, if the profession were morally wrong, they would not have held it up as an example to Christians?

CHRISTN. You shall soon see where this argument will bring you. The Apostle, who took certain illustrations from the life of a soldier, took others also from the Grecian games. 1 Cor. ix, 24, 25. If, therefore, he meant to recommend war in the one case, by parity of reasoning, he meant to recommend the Pagan games in the other. Nay, his illustration upsets your argument at once, " *they* do it", he says, " to obtain a *corruptible* crown" [not a Christian crown] " but *we* an incorruptible." Again, our Lord

Himself sets before us the example of an unjust steward.—St. Luke xvi. He proposes points in his character for our imitation. Does, therefore, the All-holy God commend injustice? But you will say, "Surely, if the character of an unjust man were morally wrong, Christ would not have held it up as an example to Christians." Injustice is quite as inseparable from an "unjust steward," as bloodshed is from a soldier. So you see the argument will not hold.

Sol. No: I grant that an argument, to be a real argument, must be consistent throughout. This will not hold; but I take one that will. When soldiers came to John, he did not tell them not to fight; he certainly told them to "do violence to no man," but that meant private acts of extortion and wrong; and he told them also to "be content with their wages".

Christn. John the Baptist was a Jew, and was speaking to Jews, and under the Jewish dispensation—the dispensation of "eye for eye, tooth for tooth, burning for burning, stripe for stripe, wound for wound." Ex. xxi, 24, 25. Fightings were of course allowed. The New Dispensation had not been promulgated when John preached. It was not till after the Resurrection, that the "kingdom of Heaven" upon earth—the least member of which was greater than the Baptist (St. Matt. xi, 11)— came with power and in its fulness. John was pre-

paring for that kingdom, not preaching its doctrines.
He taught the baptism of Repentance, as preparatory
to the Christian doctrine of Baptism; and hence, he
told the soldiers, as a necessary part of Repentance,
"to do violence to no man." Now, I hardly know
how a soldier can exercise his calling, in time of war,
without doing violence to some one. So it seems to
me you cannot get much from that argument.

Sol. You mistake the meaning of the word,
which is rendered "violence."

Christn. I beg your pardon; the word is διασειω,
which means to "shake violently," and is very well
rendered in our text; or, if you prefer it, take the
marginal reading, "*put no man in fear.*" Now,
what is your vocation at Sebastopol? Is it not to
put every man in fear with whom you come in con-
tact?

Sol. It appears to me that you lose sight of the
national in the personal. You make a general application of passages which were spoken to individuals, and you make them the ground work of
your argument against classes and wholes.

Christn. Of course I do, because persons are
not saved or damned in classes, but individually.
No number of men or nations can save your
soul, if you break the law of Christ.—Rom. xiv, 12.
"*Every one of us shall give account of himself to
God.*" If that law forbids you to steal individually,
it equally forbids you to commit the act when in

company with others. So, in like manner, when
you are commanded not to kill your brother, it matters not whether you do it alone or a thousand
others join you in the perpetration. No number of
men can relieve you of the awful talent of individual
responsibility; nor Governments justify you in the
sight of God for *voluntarily* entering upon a profession which must bring you into collision with His
laws. It is said in a Book, which you and I both
profess to respect and believe, " No man may deliver
his brother, nor make agreement unto God for him."
Ps. xlix, 7. Each, then, must stand or fall by himself.

Sol. What you say is doubtless just, if it could
be shown that the Law of God would be violated by
killing under all circumstances. Is there no such
thing as killing a man in self-defence? Suppose you
were to see a murderer killing a person on the highway, would you not go and kill the murderer, if
necessary, to deliver the oppressed? Or, if a thief
came to your house at night, would you not turn
him out?

Christn. Of course I should turn him out if I
could, but if he refused to go I would not kill him;
nor would the law exculpate me if I did. If I saw
a man committing a murder in the highway, I would
endeavour to restrain him; but, if I found him too
strong for me, I would not deprive him of life.
It could do him no good, nor myself either, to take

away his life because he had taken away the life
of another. Nor am I sure that I should kill a
man in self-defence, and St. Matt. xxvi, 52, will
bear me out. Peter drew the sword in self-defence:
but what said his Master to him? " *Put up thy
sword into thy sheath.*" Surely, if self-defence were
a principle of Christianity, innocence and virtue
might have claimed it here. I certainly should not
kill *willingly*. I mean that I would not put myself
in the way to kill. I would not go armed with revolvers and Minié rifles, rockets, Lancaster guns and
bomb-shells, as you do at Sebastopol.

Sol. We merely arm ourselves in self-defence.
From the necessities of our position, we are obliged
to use such weapons.

Christn. But what business had you in such
a position? If you run a risk, you must take the
consequence.

Sol. Pooh!

Christn. Don't sneer, but argue. If a case will
not bear the test of argument, depend upon it you
will not make it better by sneering; and, more than
that, God has given you intellect, for the use or
abuse of which you are morally responsible. Now,
intellect must lead you to say something more than
pooh! in a case of life and death.

Sol. Yes: but all persons have not the same
amount of intellect. You argue better than I do.

Christn. True: but that arises not from any deficiency of intellect on your part, but from the weakness of your case. While you attempt to do what no man has ever yet succeeded in doing, and what, in fact, no man can do—viz. *justify your position as a soldier upon the principles of Christianity or from the Christian Scriptures*—you must expect to fail in argument.

Sol. But I have never heard that war in the present state of things is contrary to the principles of Christianity.

Christn. What is the principle of war?

Sol. A just war is undertaken in self-defence, and its principle is of course resistance to aggression.

Christn. We need not particularize as to *just* and unjust war, for every nation which goes to war believes in the justice of its cause; and consequently what is *just* in the eyes of one man, one government, one nation, is unjust in the eyes of another man, another government, another nation. Defensive wars become aggressive in their turn (witness the Crimean and Baltic expeditions), and aggressive wars become defensive. But the *principle of all war* is retaliation for wrong done, is it not?

Sol. Unquestionably it is: if there were no national wrong, there would be no national wars.

Christn. Now, what is the principle of Christianity, but the reverse of retaliation? "If a man smite thee on the one cheek, turn the other also." St. Luke vi, 29. Is that the principle of war?

"Ye have heard that it hath been said, An eye for an eye, and a tooth for a tooth; but I say unto you, that ye resist not evil." Is that retaliation? Again, "Ye have heard that it hath been said, Thou shalt love thy neighbour, and hate thine enemy; but I say unto you, love your enemies; bless them that curse you; do good to them that hate you; and pray for them that despitefully use you." St. Matt. v. 38, &c. Is this war, or anything approaching to the principle of war—nay, is it not the exact reverse? Can you love your enemy while cutting his throat, or pray for him while plunging a pike into his body? You say you are going to *avenge* the blood of your brethren who fell at Alma and Inkerman; and the letters which reach us from the seat of war describe the army as impatient for revenge. Is that Christianity? Turn to Romans xii : "Dearly beloved, avenge not yourselves, but rather give place unto wrath; for it is written, Vengeance is mine, I will repay, saith the Lord. Therefore, if thine enemy hunger, feed him; if he thirst, give him drink." Rom. xii, 19, 20. Is this the spirit which animates our soldiery in the trenches before Sebastopol, or on the plains of Inkerman? And if it applies to individual cases between man and man, does it the less apply to aggregates made up of these individuals? Does a man lose his moral responsibility by mixing in bad company? But still further; the essential principle of Christianity is *love*. In love to us Christ became incarnate, Gal. iv, 4, 5, 6.—In love to us He died on Calvary, St. John, xv, 13; Rom. v, 8.—In love to us He ascended to the mansions of glory, St. John, xvi, 7. You know the inference, for an Apostle has drawn it. "Beloved, if God so loved us, we ought also to love one another," 1 St. John, iv, 11. "If a man say, I love God, and hateth his brother, he is a liar; for if he loveth not his brother whom he hath seen, how can he love God whom he hath not seen?" "And this commandment we have from Him, That he who loveth God, loves his brother also," Ch. v, 20, 21. Moreover, the same Apostle says in another place, Ch. iii, 15: "Whosoever hateth his brother is a murderer." What would he say to the slayer of his brother? Now, I contend, and any impartial mind must see, that all these passages, whether of individual or of universal application, are both in spirit and in letter opposed to retaliation, revenge, bloodshed—in a word, to war.

Sol. But do you not think that the love which the Gospel commends is love for men's souls rather than for their bodies?

Christn. For both soul and body. When the Samaritans would not receive our Lord, you may remember that James and John asked Him, if they should call down fire from heaven and consume their ungrateful neighbours, as was done before by one of God's servants under the Old Dispensation? St. Luke, ix, 54, &c. They quoted Scripture, you perceive (2 Kings, 1). Our Lord's reply to this request is a perfect answer to those who would carry fire and sword into a neighbouring country, because of some wrong inflicted by individuals of that country, whether princes or peasants, and then appeal to the Scriptures of the Old Testament in justification. While admitting the fact that Elias had done so, Jesus turned, says the faithful Evangelist, and rebuked the disciples James and John, saying, " Ye know not what manner of spirit ye are of. For the Son of Man is not come to destroy men's lives, but to save them." And I would seriously ask the Warners, the Dundonalds, the Neilsons, and other inventors of ' infernal machines'—the Miniès, and Colts, and Lancasters, whom our Christian (?) governments now hold in such high admiration, to consider what manner of spirit they are of. But further, what was our Lord's whole life but a perpetual healing of men's bodies, and what the lives of His Apostles? Ought we not, then, to follow their example so far as we can; and, instead of maiming and mutilating that body, which He took, and by taking, blest, learn to reverence and respect it for His sake?

SOL.   I think we ought: but am I to understand you that the command to love all men is absolute?

CHRISTN.   Certainly.   On what grounds do you doubt it?

SOL.   Because Christ says that we are to treat

some men as heathens and publicans. St. Matt. xviii, 17. And Peter struck Ananias and Sapphira dead for telling a lie; and St. Paul delivered Hymenæus and Alexander to Satan. So it seems to me that the argument from universal love, as an absolute command, will not hold.

CHRISTN. Yes, it will; and the cases which you have adduced strengthen it. The treating a man as a heathen and a publican, *i. e.*, setting him apart from the congregation, was clearly an act of love to his soul; just as St. Paul's was towards Hymenæus and Alexander, whom he delivered to Satan to be afflicted for a time, says Doddridge, with pains and sickness, " that they may learn not to blaspheme"; in other words, that they may be drawn to repentance. In both cases the discipline was correctional, as all Christian discipline is. Heb. xii, 7. The case of the incestuous person at Corinth is directly to the point. When St. Paul commanded the congregation to withdraw from him (1 Cor. v, 13), it was for the sake of bringing him to repentance; which had no sooner been effected, than the Apostle writes back to the brethren to receive him again, to " forgive him and comfort him", lest " he should be swallowed up with overmuch sorrow." " Wherefore I beseech you that ye would confirm your *love* towards him." 2 Cor. ii, 7, 8. It was love, then, for his immortal soul which suggested the punishment. Now, will you undertake to say, that our

mission to Sebastopol to punish our Russian brothers
is of the same character, or dictated by the same
spirit? Are you going to use your sword and rifle
that "your brother's soul may be saved in the day
of the Lord"? You know you are not. You know
that as soon as you get into the trenches, the first
Russian who shows his head above a rifle-pit will
have a bullet through it from your rifle, or it will
not be your fault. Nay, if the destiny of his immortal soul depended upon your trigger, you know
you would not slack your hand; for you have gone
there to kill irrespective of all consequences to the
slaughtered; that ribbons and clasps will be your
reward, and the more you fight like a tiger than a
man, the more decorated you will be.

As regards St. Peter, what he did, you and I
cannot do. He saw the wickedness of Ananias's and
Sapphira's heart, and, inspired by the Spirit, pronounced God's sentence against them. The sentence
was executed from heaven. God was the executioner, not Peter. The Apostle had neither spear
nor sword, save the sword of the Spirit, and Ananias's
sin was not against a fellow mortal; was neither an
encroachment upon Turkey, nor the fortifying of
Sebastopol, but a sin against the Holy Ghost. I
hope you consider this a complete answer to your
question. If not, be good enough to show wherein
its incompleteness lies.

Sol. I suppose your argument is unanswerable;

at least, I see no way of escape. But yet it seems strange that God should do a thing that is wrong in itself.

CHRISTN. That which is right in God to do, may be very wrong in us. God judges the thoughts and intents of men, but dare we attempt to do so? " Samuel hewed Agag in pieces before the Lord in Gilgal," 1 Sam. xv. 33. Does it therefore follow that we are justified in committing murder?

SOL. Certainly not; but is there any direct command against killing which is to be considered of universal application?

CHRISTN. *" Do not kill."* St. Mark x, 19; St. Luke xviii, 20. And St. James ii, 11, " He that said, Do not commit adultery, said also, Do not kill. Now if thou commit no adultery, yet if thou kill, thou art become a transgressor of the law."

SOL. This does look as if the command were absolute; because if not absolute in the one case, it cannot be held absolute in the other. I mean that it must apply to the sixth and seventh commandments equally. But how then does it come to pass that these commands should be regarded as absolute, and yet killing under certain conditions be allowed?

CHRISTN. I say that under the Jewish dispensation the command not to kill was anything but absolute. There were exceptional cases expressly provided for. So there were also exceptional cases to the seventh commandment, both as a permission,

Deut. xxi, 10, 11, and as a punishment, 2 Sam. xii, 8, 11 ; Jer. vi, 12 ; viii, 10. But Christ in adopting these moral commands into His dispensation perfected them by making them absolute. Matt. xix, 8, 9 ; Gal. iii, 24 ; Jas. ii, 11.

Sol. I see the force of this ; and I am much struck by your general argument, and my mind is, I think, undergoing a change on the subject. I wish, however, for more information ; for some opinions of the earlier Christian writers—Fathers as you call them ; because I have read somewhere, perhaps in Tertullian, that so far back as his days, Christians fought in the Roman armies. That they did under Constantine, and preceding emperors, there can be no doubt.

Christn. I shall be very happy to give you such information as I possess, scanty though it be ; but I suppose we need not speak of times so late as Constantine's, when the Church adopted into her service not only the weapons but the policy of the world.* The extracts which I shall give, will show

---

* "It was now," says Milman (the present Dean of St. Paul's) "it was now, *for the first time* (three hundred years after the Christian era), that the meek and peaceful Jesus became a God of battle ; and the cross, the holy sign of Christian redemption, a banner of bloody strife. This *irreconcileable incongruity* between the symbol of universal peace and the horrors of war, in my judgment, is conclusive against the miraculous or supernatural character of the transaction,—viz. the vision which resulted in the adoption of the cross as a symbol of war." "And," adds the Dean, in a note, " I was agreeably surprised

how fully these fine old fellows—the Fathers—imbibed the spirit of Christianity, and the contrast of their religion with that of the majority of modern Christians.

Tertullian, who died at a very great age about the year 216, in commenting on the third chapter of St. Luke and the fourteenth verse says, "Though soldiers came to John and received their rule of duty, and even though a centurion was a believer, the Lord in disarming Peter *thenceforward disarmed every soldier*"; and he goes on also to say, that even the dress of a soldier is unlawful for a Christian. "No dress is lawful for us which is assigned to an unlawful action."

Justin Martyr, who wrote his famous Apology to Antoninus Pius in the year 139, quotes from Isaiah to show that Christianity was to be a religion of peace not war, and what the duties of Christians were. "Nation shall not lift up sword against nation, neither shall they learn war any more", &c. Wherefore," he says, "we who *formerly killed* one another, now not only *abstain from fighting against our enemies*", &c. Again, sec. 49, "We who hated and killed one another, and permitted not those of another nation to live with us, now live at the same table and *pray for our enemies.*" "Our Master

to find that Mosheim concurred in these sentiments; for which I will readily encounter the charge of Quakerism."—*Hist. Christ.*, b. ii, p. 354.

taught us to endure all evil, to turn one cheek and then the other", &c.

St. Chrysostom, on Matt. xxvi, 55—where the Jews came with swords to take our Lord, and Judas kissed Him—says, against harsh treatment in general, " How wilt thou receive the sacred Host when thou hast corrupted thy tongue with human gore; how give the kiss of peace with mouth gorged with war !"

Again, in St. Luke xxii: "Say not that such a one murdered such a one, and that is why I turn away from him; for, even if he were upon the point of thrusting a sword down into thee, and to plunge his hand into thy neck, kiss this very hand." Is this the principle of war?

St. Ambrose, on the words, "Shall we smite with the sword"—St. Luke, xxii, 49, says, the Lord prophesied that the Apostles, *forgetful of the gifts and Law of Christ*, would dare to take up the sword." In the opinion of St. Ambrose then, a man has forgotten the Law of Christ when he dares to take up the sword. But his own life was a commentary upon the text. Not to speak of his refusal to allow the Emperor Theodosius even to enter a church for eight months, because he had ordered the slaughter of his subjects in an insurrection, and out of revenge; the historian tells us, that "under the influence of Ambrose, this—the last great Emperor of the World—refrained for a time from communicating in the Christian mysteries [the Sacrament of the Lord's Supper] because his hands were stained with blood, though that blood had been shed in *a just and necessary war.*" (Milman, *History of Christianity*, b. iii, p. 262). And I believe it was owing to Ambrose that the Statue of Victory was dragged from the pedestal in the Senate-house—the altar removed and the worship proscribed, before that of any other Statue. This is anything but an insignificant fact. It called forth the wonder of the historian in these words : *one " would have thought that all other statues would have been thrown prostrate, all other worship proscribed, before that of victory."* Yes, a soldier would have thought so, certainly, but not a follower of Him who said ; " My kingdom is not of this world ; if my kingdom were of this world, then would my servants fight," St. John xviii, 36. And, to come even to later times, long after Christianity had become corrupted, we find Erasmus saying :—" They who defend war, must defend the dispositions which lead to war : *and these dispositions are absolutely forbidden.*"

Sol. But is it not a fact, that soldiers who were called and recognized as Christians, were enrolled in the Roman Legions long before the days of Constantine? Tertullian (now that I remember the passage) certainly does say to the Roman governors, that so far from the Christians being few in number, they filled all places of the Roman Empire,—' cities,

B

islands, castles, corporations, councils, *armies*, tribes, companies, the palace, the Senate and the courts of judicature.' Apol. c. 37.

CHRISTN. Obviously, much of this must be hyperbole: Christians did not *fill* all, or *fill* any of these. If so, the record of the persecutions attributed to Nero, Domitian, Diocletian, and others, must be absurd; unless you believe that Christians persecuted and slaughtered Christians. That Christians were found in senates, courts, armies, is all that this Apology proves; and is all, I suppose, that you contend for. But Tertullian did not tell you what sort of Christians they were who were found in armies, did he? He does moreover say, and so do Justin Martyr and Irenæus; nay, even so do the Apostles themselves—St. Paul, St. John, St. Jude and St. Peter,—that there were many bad Christians among them from the very first; Philip. i, 16; Jo. iii, 9, 10; Jude 4; 2 Pet. ii. Even Pliny, a Pagan and an enemy, in his letter to the Emperor Trajan, A.D. 107, reports the same. "Others," he says: "mentioned in the libel, confessed themselves Christians, but presently denied it; that they had been such, but had renounced it some three years ago; others, many years, and one as far back as five-and-twenty years ago. All of whom paid their reverence and veneration to your statue and the images of the gods, *and blasphemed Christ.*"

In the Diocletian persecutions we are told, (vide

Cave's Lives) that the war of extermination waged by this Emperor against the Christians, was so hot, that the very framework of society was unhinged by it;—Christians informed against Christians; children against parents and friends against their friends. Probably it was to such Christians that Tertullian alluded, when he said they " filled" the Roman armies. What sort of Christians they must have been, we gather from the oath administered to the soldiers on their enrolment, viz. : to fight for their country and for the religion of the gods and the person of the Emperor. Symbolum—the Latin word for our 'Creed,' signifies, it is said, this oath or watchword, " whereby the soldiers of the same camp were known from their enemies." Catechism Edward VI, 1552.

If you use the argument from Tertullian as a proof that fighting was not incompatible with Christianity, you will find that it proves too much. It proves also, that idolatry was not ; and that to deny Christ before men (St. Matt. x, 33), was not incompatible either. For most assuredly, had these soldiers been suspected of being Christians, they would have been forced to sacrifice to the gods—or, would have been beheaded. We do not hear that they were beheaded or reckoned among the martyrs of that period; therefore they must have sacrificed, or remained undiscovered,—protecting idolatry and denying Christ. In fact, when Diocletian did all that man and Satan could do to exterminate Christianity from his dominions;—when through ten long bloody years, he murdered and proscribed the disciples of Christ wherever they could be found,—do you think that he would have spared any of the soldiers, who should dare to profess a religion contrary to their oath and his imperial will, and who sought to overthrow the established worship of their country? And moreover, it must be remembered, that (admitting Tertullian to be right as to his statistics) the Christians were quite strong enough then to have taken up arms in self-defence—your principle. They did not do so; therefore, Tertullian is wrong—or, to take up arms in self-defence is no part of Christianity. Leaving you to extricate yourself from the horns of this dilemma, I will quote again Tertullian's own words as an answer to those who bring him forward to advocate the cause of *Christian soldiers!* " Though soldiers came to John and received their rule of duty, &c., yet Christ, in disarming Peter, *thenceforward disarmed every soldier.*"

Sol. Do you know any individual cases in which Christians in early times refused to fight because they were Christians?

Christn. Yes, many; I will give you a few well-known instances.* Maximilian was brought before

* Vide "Rights and Obligations of Mankind," Essay iii, p. 182.

the Tribunal to be enrolled as a soldier. On the Proconsul's asking his name, he replied, 'I am a Christian and cannot fight.' He was told, there was no alternative between enrolment and death. "I cannot fight," he said, "if I die, for I am a Christian." He remained stedfast and was consigned to the executioner.

Marcellus, while holding a centurion's commission in the legion called Trajana, became a Christian, and believing—in common with his fellow-Christians, that war was not lawful for him, threw down his belt or girdle at the head of his legion, declaring that he would serve no longer; for that "it was not lawful for a Christian to bear arms for any earthly consideration." He was put to death.

Cassian, a notary to the same legion, relinquished his office for the same reason, and like Marcellus, was consigned to the executioner. Martin, a much celebrated soldier in his day, embraced Christianity and gave up his commission. He was brought before Julian the Apostate, "I am a Christian," said he, "and therefore I cannot fight."

Tatian says, that "the Christians declined even military commands." Lactantius, that it can *never* be lawful for a righteous man to go to war. Celsus, a Pagan, charged the Christians with *refusing to bear arms, even in cases of necessity*. Origen admits the charge, because *war was unlawful*.* Surely there

* *Ibid.* Vide also "Testimony of the Early Christians against War," by T. Clarkson, M.A.

is no necessity for pursuing this point further? If there were, I might tell you of the Paterines or Cazari of Italy, in the eleventh, twelfth and thirteenth centuries,—in the midst of the Crusades—who " held that it was not lawful to bear arms or to kill mankind.''

Sol. Your allusion to the Crusades, reminds me of a question I wanted to put some time back. And I ask it now lest I should forget it. Is there any early canon or decree of council on the subject?

Christn. There is: the twelfth canon of the Council of Nice—a council recognized and received by the Church of England — decrees that " Inasmuch as some, who have been called by grace and have at first displayed their ardour and laid aside their belts [or girdles], have returned again like dogs to their vomit, and have spent their money in purchasing again a place in the army,—they must continue amongst the prostrators for ten years, after having been three years amongst the hearers,"—*i.e.* thirteen years penance before they could be allowed to communicate, or be received into the body of the faithful.

That " some learned persons are of opinion that the Ancients had so much dislike to the military life as to excommunicate such as bore arms after baptism," even Bingham *admits*. And it is a well-known fact that Constantine, who presided at the Council of Nice, was not baptized during the time of his bearing arms. He was baptized on his death-bed, more than twenty years after his so-called conversion, during all which time he was more or less engaged in war. I do not say this *was* his reason for putting off his baptism ; it may have been."

SOL. But, if the Church of England receives the decrees of this Council, of which there can be no doubt, how is the canon to be interpreted, for her Thirty-seventh Article apparently contradicts it ?

CHRISTN. There are two interpretations of the Article. The first is, that the Article alludes only to *just* wars — a point on which you may satisfy yourself by referring to the original language of the Article :—" Christianis licet ex mandato magistratus arma portare et *justa bella* administrare". This version, observe, is quite as authentic as the English version, and in fact explains it. " *The Articles of 1562 were drawn up in Latin only*, but in 1571 they were subscribed by the members of the two houses of Convocation both in Latin and English, and *there-fore the Latin and English copies are to be considered as equally authentic.*"* Now once consent to limit the bearing of arms to *just* wars, and you will soon find that all wars undertaken for political purposes, or territorial aggrandisement, that is to say, all of national origin are practically excluded. For "*just*" must mean "*just*" in His sight who weighs nations

* Tomlin's Christian Theology, vol. ii. p. 35

in the balance of infinite rectitude, and not in the
mere opinion of a Foreign Minister who chooses to
think every war just, in which he feels a disposition
to engage. All civilised nations that go to war
make justice their plea, and appeal to Heaven to
defend their cause on this ground. Are there then
two just sides to a quarrel?—one the exact opposite of the other. Yet, unless you claim infalli-
bility—the prerogative of God alone—and you ought
to claim nothing less when you take upon yourself
to people the Eternal World with immortal souls
and deluge the earth with human blood. Now can
you be *sure* that justice is in reality on the side
which you espouse, or that God looks at the case in
the same light as you do?

The other interpretation is, that the Article refers
to matters of law—the law of the realm—rather
than to matters of conscience. And the language
of some of our most eminent divines appears to
favour this interpretation. That they could *not
have understood the Article as sanctioning war in
a religious view* is obvious enough. Bishop Jeremy
Taylor writes, "War *is as contrary to the Christian
religion, as cruelty is to mercy, tyranny to charity.**
Bishop Watson, that "war has practices and principles peculiar to itself, which but ill quadrate
with the rule of *moral rectitude,* and are *quite ab-*

* Vide "War, &c.", a sermon preached at St. Andrew's,
Wells-street, by the Rev. A. B. Evans, March 1855.

horrent from the benignity of Christianity."* Would then, these excellent and eminent divines have upheld that which they assert to be " contrary to the Christian religion, to the rule of moral rectitude, and abhorrent to the benignity of Christianity ?" Would they appeal to the article, in justification, as a religious question, of that which, as a religious question, they so emphatically condemned ? Southey again, who wrote a book in defence and support of the Church, says, " There is but one community of Christians, enlightened enough to understand the prohibition of war by our divine Master, in its plain, literal and *undeniable sense*, and conscientious enough to obey it, subduing the very instincts of Nature to obedience."†

Dr. Vicissimus Knox says, "*morality and religion* forbid war in its motives, conduct and consequences."‡

But it is needless to multiply authorities, for as Mr. Evans well observes, in his Sermon on " War : its Theology, its Anomalies, its Incidents, and its Humiliations," (Lumley) which for vigour of expression, and force of argument, I commend to your quiet reading ; it is not to be supposed that the Article contravenes the Gospel, or means to assert,

* Life of Bishop Watson.
† Southey's " History of Brazil."
‡ " Essays." For the above, and many other authorities, vide "Rights and Obligations of Mankind," Essay iii, ch. xix.

as a doctrine, that which is contrary to its letter and spirit.

Sol. But had not the canon, which you quoted, reference to local matters,—to the times when soldiers were dismissed for not worshipping the gods ? And is there no canon of that period, ordering Christians to fight ?

Christn. I do not know, nor do you, that the canon had any reference to the question you propose. Up to that time no Council had decreed that Christians were to fight. The spirit of Christianity forbad those passions and dispositions, apart from which, War could not exist; and Christians were too pure and uncorrupt then to decree any thing in the opposite spirit. But when, as I said, the Church began to adopt into her service the policy of the world, a canon was procured, under questionable influence, at Arles, excommunicating such as "threw away their *arms in time of peace*, on pretence that *they were Christians*," Con. Arelat, 1 Can. 3. And it is most probable that the Great Œcumenical Council of Nice, held a few years after the Provincial Council of Arles, had reference to this as well as to other Provincial Canons, and repealed it.by a general decree. The important fact, however, which the Council of Arles proves, is that *Christians did consider it contrary to their profession to bear arms, even in time of peace.* This testimony completes my Argument from Antiquity.

PART II.

THE ARGUMENT CONTINUED INDEPENDENT OF THE
LETTER OF SCRIPTURE; AND ILLUSTRATIONS OF
THE SPIRIT OF WAR, AND THE SPIRIT OF
CHRISTIANITY.

———

Sol. I am happy to meet you again; for my
mind has undergone a considerable change on the
subject of our last conversation; and you will no
doubt be glad to hear it. I am convinced now, of
what I once thought I never should be convinced,
—because, perhaps, I never seriously reflected upon
the matter—and that is, that *war and Christianity
are in principle essential opposites ;* and therefore,
the better warrior, or greater hero a man becomes,
the worst Christian he must necessarily be; and I
am led to this conclusion, as much by the spirit of
those passages which you quoted from the New Testament, as by direct argument. If my father had
given the subject a little more consideration when

he purchased my commission, I should not now
have to begin the world anew ; but do so I will,
for my commission will be in the market (since the
Commander-in-Chief will not accept my resignation
absolutely) before to-morrow night. I will not go
to Sebastopol, come what may, nor draw a sword
against any poor child of mortality more. I cannot
shake the words out of my mind, " what is a man
profited if he shall gain the whole world and lose
his own soul?" St. Matt. xvi.

CHRISTN.   Your firmness and decision are now
moulding you into the good soldier of Christ, (2
Tim. ii. 3), and forming the character which St.
Paul commends. Follow up, then, your present train
of thought, and you will be guided aright, I have no
doubt.   And I would urge you not to look at Christianity merely from disjointed texts or abstract passages ; but to view it in its general tenor and bearing
—in a word, its *spirit*.   Regard it as the antidote of
passion and violence, whether in the concrete or the
abstract ; whether in individual units or in masses
of units ; whether in one man or in a million of men,
which in fact it is; look upon it as the grand inculca-
tor of forbearance and forgiveness, benevolence and
love, and your conviction that the spirit of war is the
spirit which Christianity prohibits, will be forcibly
strengthened.   When men ask for a 'Thus saith
the Lord,' if such passages as I quoted will not satisfy,
tell them that the New Testament was not drawn

up as a register of every sin which it is possible for man to commit,—and which, in its very nature and essence it prohibits. It nowhere, save by implication, forbids suicide, infanticide, polygamy or manslaughter; yet no one doubts that these crimes are forbidden. If the command *not to kill* is not absolute, who is to draw the line? If the command is, as the war advocates tell us, only confined to acts of private revenge between man and man, what of infanticide? And surely I have as much reason to believe that the command does not apply to self-destruction, as you have, that it does not apply to national destruction. If the latter is not an act of private revenge, most assuredly the other is not.

Will any one justify robbery, because our Lord does not reprobate the conduct of the thieves, in the parable of the Good Samaritan? Christ simply says, "A certain man went down from Jerusalem to Jericho and fell among thieves, who stripped him of his raiment and wounded him, leaving him half dead." St. Luke x, 30,—not a word of condemnation—nor even a hint *directly*, that thieving and wounding are wrong. Now, why is this? Why, but that Christ did not,—nor was it necessary that He should,—define always what is wrong. He lays down great principles, *which tell us always what is right*. Mercy, forbearance, gentleness, meekness, purity of heart, endurance of wrong, peacemaking,

are the principles which He everywhere inculcates.
Retaliation, resentment, destruction, bloodshed, in-
juries, are the principles of war. Both cannot exist
together. If you say, that Christians, while engaged in the destruction of life and property, only
suspend the principle of non-injury, of gentleness, of
love—as has been said, you simply assert what I have
been saying all along, that while we engage in war
we abandon Christianity. And thus the advocates
of war are driven into this corner, from whence, I
confess, I see no escape, viz.—that the Gospel allows
a man to be a Christian to-day and a savage to-
morrow, and a Christian again the next day, and
something else the day after.—That it permits him
to go upon his knees and intreat for forgiveness at
God's hand, *because* he "forgives them that trespass
against" him and his; and, in the next breath, to
rise from his knees, beat his regiment to arms, and
blow out the brains of those who have so trespassed;
that it obliges him one minute to believe that he
"who keeps the whole law and yet offendeth in one
point, is guilty of all," St. James ii, 10, and permits
him the next, by the very permission of war, to
violate, not only every command of the Decalogue,
but every moral sentiment as well. For I have
never yet heard of a war, in which Sabbath-breaking,
profane swearing, killing, fornicating or worse,
stealing (pillage), treachery (outwitting), and covet-
ousness, "which is idolatry," Colos. iii, 5, were not

openly perpetrated; and, if not justified, at least excused, on the theory that such are inseparable from the evils of war? And if inseparable, then what of the principles which develope into such crimes? The greatest warrior of the age is reported to have said, in his place in Parliament, when discussing the proposal to increase the army chaplains, that " IT WILL NOT DO TO MAKE SOLDIERS TOO RELIGIOUS." Was there not then in his mind some necessary connexion between war and immorality?

SOL. Certainly the argument on your side is most convincing; and it strikes me that those who defend the opposite side have a personal interest in so doing. In defending war, it is themselves—their prejudices and feelings—they are defending; and you know very well that the desire of self-justification often prompts one to give importance to arguments which, when calmly considered, are as weak as possible.

CHRISTN. Yes, it is particularly so in this case. It seems to me that those who believe war not to be contrary to Christianity must be persons *who never think.* Surely a little reflection would show that it is impossible to admit the essential principles of war as a moral obligation, and, at the same time, be a believer in the essential doctrines of Christianity. You must give up one or the other *ex necessitate rei.* Consider for a moment what the essential doctrines of Christianity are:—1st. Immortality of the soul.

2nd. The resurrection of the body. 3rd. The pater-
nity of God, &c. Can you suppose, then, that the
inventors and advocates of shells, torpedos, rockets,
Miniés, Lancasters and other infernal machines, *really*
believe that souls hurried suddenly into eternity (the
express object of these missiles), and unprepared,
will be for ever consigned to a place of misery? If
so, what sort of love, what sort of *humanity* must
theirs be, leaving Christianity out of the question
altogether? Can you suppose the belief in the resurrection of the body to be in any way compatible
with sending that body to the grave a mutilated and
mangled corpse? Can any one *really* believe (what
Christianity alone reveals) that God is "Our Father",
and that He regards us all as one family, descended
from one common stock, and warmed by kindred
blood; and at the same time pray to Him to assist
one half of His family in butchering the other half?
The very idea is profane, and yet it is one that is
acted upon every day.

Sol. No doubt, to a candid and reflective mind,
the argument, independent of the letter of the New
Testament, is irresistible; and I believe that all I
have heard advanced on the other side (now I come
to consider the matter), may be summed up in the
one word "utilitarian"; that is to say, were we to
possess no soldiers, what would become of us as a
nation; and what is the use of soldiers, if they are
not to fight?

CHRISTN. All which means, if we fear God and keep His commandments, what will become of us? I, for one, am content to leave the result to Him. "Utilitarian" is the word. We have rights, it is said, as citizens of a nation (which, by the way, we learnt from Aristotle and other pagan moralists); and these, or whatever we imagine to be such, though relating only to this world, or the few short years we may be in it, are to take precedence of the laws of Christ:—the laws of intellectual, moral, and individual responsibility, which are in their very nature eternal! Of what use is Christianity, if it is to do no more for nations, as nations, than Paganism or Judaism has done in this respect? The very existence of soldiers under the Christian dispensation seems to me an egregious anomaly. And touching their *use*, I could, if I had not already exhausted your patience, give you some statistics that would almost make your hair stand on end ; statistics of millions upon millions of the human race hurried into eternity, reeking with passion and blood—victims of the demon of war ;—of millions upon millions of money squandered in the prosecution of this destruction—money that might have evangelized the the globe, and have raised the social condition of every living being ;—have founded schools in every village in the world, and furnished churches for a thousand millions of worshippers. But not to go back to the past, let me give a few items for reflection connected with the war in which we are at this moment engaged.

During the past year, England alone has spent £40,000,000 upon the demon, and sacrificed Twenty-seven Thousand of her sons at his shrine. France has spent of course an equal sum (since the expenses of the war are to be divided between us), and sacrificed of her sons Sixty and Six Thousand!! that is to say, upwards of Ninety Thousand immortal souls of England and France alone have been, more or less suddenly, sent to the bar of the God of Peace, to justify their passions and their perpetrations there! On the Russian side, since this war began, 250,000, and on the Turkish, 120,000, according to Lord Grey's speech in the House of Lords, have gone also. "Can any of us," says that nobleman, "look upon such a fearful waste of life without shuddering? Five Hundred Thousand human beings have been sacrificed to the grim idol of war, and as yet it has not lasted two years." But to confine myself to matters more nearly connected with our late exploits, I will give you, on the one hand, proofs of that spirit which war engenders, both in those engaged in it and those who advocate it; and, on the other hand, a few quotations from the book which both parties profess to believe.

Times, June 1855.
"Lord Panmure presents his compliments to the editor of

Epis. ad Corinth. A.D. 57.
St. Paul, writing to the Co-rinthians, says, "Now I rejoice

The Times, and has GREAT PLEASURE in transmitting the enclosed intelligence:

"'*June* 8.

"'The success of last night was very complete......*Nothing could be more brilliant* than the advance of our allies. *We* have lost about 400 men, killed and wounded.'"

[Not a word of sorrow.]

"'The public buildings, &c., have been burnt.'"

[What a *cause* of great pleasure!]

"*June* 8.

"The Secretary of the Admiralty presents his compliments to the editor of *The Times,* and has GREAT PLEASURE in forwarding a copy of the enclosed:

"'The public buildings and numerous government magazines of provisions have been burnt, and thus *an immense loss of supplies has been inflicted on the enemy.*"

"Lord Panmure presents," &c., "and has GREAT PLEASURE in transmitting the enclosed intelligence:

"'The formidable fire which began yesterday was kept up with the greatest spirit....The whole operation' [of carrying the Mamelon] 'was most brilliant. Casualties not known.'"

"The slaughter," says another telegraph, "*was* fearful"!!

[This, of course, was of trifling importance compared with the *great pleasure* of taking a mound of earth and stones.]

Let us now see in what spirit

not *that ye were made sorry.*" (2 Cor. vii, 9.)

"*As ye would that men should do to you, do ye also to them likewise. But love ye your enemies, and do good.*" (St. Luke, vi, 31, 35.)

"*Put up thy sword into his place; for all they that take the sword, shall perish with the sword.*" (St. Matt. xxvi, 52.)

"*Lord, wilt Thou that we command fire to come down from heaven, and consume them, as Elias did? But he turned and rebuked them, and said, Ye know not what manner of spirit ye are of; for the Son of Man is not come to destroy men's lives, but to save them.*"(S.Luke ix,54-56.)

"*Recompense to no man evil for evil....Therefore, if thine enemy hunger, feed him; if he thirst, give him drink. Be not overcome of evil, but overcome evil with good.*" (Rom. xii, 17.)

"*Ye have heard that it hath been said, thou shalt love thy neighbour, and hate thine enemy. But I say unto you, love your enemies; for if ye love them which love you, what reward have ye? Do not even the Publicans the same?*" (St. Matt. v.)

"*Weep with them that weep.*" (Rom. xii, 15.)

"*See that none render evil for evil unto any man, but ever follow that which is good.*" (1 Thess. v, 15.)

"*Hereby perceive we the love*

this "brilliant success" was achieved.

From the *Herald* correspondent at the seat of war :

"Then commenced a fight for its possession" [the trench] "such as has not, for ferocity and bloodshed, been equalled during the siege...By mere dint of *bayonetting and stabbing,* the French managed," &c.,&c. "The French were now thoroughly roused, and, *bent upon revenge,* followed and bayonetted the fugitives" [who had thrown away their arms.] "The total loss to the Russians is supposed to be from 1,000 to 1,500 killed and wounded, the greater part of whom were *killed, as no quarter was given*"!

Gracious heavens! No quarter given by Christians to brother Christians! No; not so much as time to say, "God, be merciful to me, a sinner!" though those Christians were unarmed, helpless, and fugitives. And this *The Guardian* calls "a very interesting account!!"

"You want to know more of the way," says a published letter from the trenches, "we actually fight...Well, first a volley, a cheer, and then the bayonet, which, first parrying (if required) our enemy's thrust, is *driven to the socket* through any part of the body we can reach, the upper part the better. Does not that seem dreadful to you at home? And, no doubt, so it is; and cursed be

of God, because he laid down his life for us; and we ought to lay down our lives for the brethren." (1 St. John iii.)

"*Resist not evil; have peace one with another; be gentle, showing all meekness unto all men. Be all of one mind, having compassion one of another, for God hath called us to peace.*" (Matth. v, 39; Mark ix, 50; Tit. iii, 2; 1 Pet. iii, 8; 1 Cor. vii, 15.)

"*Avenge not yourselves. Vengeance is mine; I will repay, saith the Lord.*" (Rom. xii, 19.)

"*A new commandment I give unto you, that ye love one another: as I have loved you, that ye also love one another. By this shall all men know that ye are my disciples, if ye have love one to another.*" (St. John xiii, 34-35.)

"*Love as brethren; be pitiful, be courteous.*" (1 Pet. iii, 8.)

"*But as touching brotherly love, ye have no need that I write unto you; for ye yourselves* are taught of God to LOVE ONE ANOTHER." (1 Thess. iv, 9.)

"*Let all bitterness and wrath and anger be put away from you, with all malice, and be ye kind one to another, tenderhearted, forgiving one another; even as God, for Christ's sake, hath forgiven you. Be ye, therefore, followers of God, as dear children, and walk in love. He that loveth not, knoweth not God. If we love one another, God dwelleth in us, and his love is perfected in us. If a man say,*

he that causes it. But in BAT-
TLE OUR FEELINGS ARE DIFFE-
RENT : the passion to kill and
destroy is raised within us ; our
blood BOILS FOR REVENGE......
The demon of war is within
you, and the work of death is
but short."

What a noble fellow ! I fancy
I hear on all sides. What a
splendid hero ! That's the stuff
the "red devils" are made of !
Have we not reason to be proud
of our country, when represented by such fine fellows ?
Yes,—I seem anxious to say,
But what of your Christianity ?

That no part of the heroic
character is the subject of the
"commendation, or precepts, or
example of Christ," even Paley
admits ; but the character the
most opposite to the heroic is
the subject of them all. (Vide
"Evidences of Christianity,"
p. 2, sec. 2.)

———

SACKING OF KERTCH.
(*Times' Correspondent.*)
"May 25.

"The French were running
riot, breaking in doors, pursuing hens, smashing windows,—
in fact, 'plundering'; *in which
they were also assisted by all of
our men who could get away.
Every* house we entered, was
ransacked.

*I love God, and hateth his bro-
ther, he is a liar; for he that
loveth not his brother, whom he
hath seen, how can he love God
whom he hath not seen ? Whosoever hateth his brother is a
murderer; and ye know that no
murderer hath eternal life abid-
ing in him. Let no man say,
when he is tempted, I am tempted
of God; for God cannot be
tempted with evil : neither
tempteth he any man. But every
man is tempted when he is
drawn away of his own lust and
enticed. Then, when lust hath
conceived, it bringeth forth sin;
and sin, when it is finished,
bringeth forth* DEATH." (Ephes.
iv, 31, &c. ; 1 John iv, 7, &c. ;
iii, 15 ; James i, 13, 14, 15.)

"*Put on . . bowels of mercies, kindness, humbleness of
mind, meekness, longsuffering :
forbearing one another and
forgiving one onother, if any
man have a quarrel against
any . . . and let the peace of
God rule in your hearts.*"
(Colos. iii. 12, 13. 15.)

"*Do not steal. Ye do wrong,
and defraud your brethren.
Let him that stole, steal no more;
but rather let him labour, working with his hands the thing
which is good. Blessed is he
that considereth the poor and
needy: the Lord will deliver
him in the time of trouble.*"
(Ephes. iv, 25 ; Mark x, 19 ;
1 Cor. vi, 8 ; Ps. xli, 1.)

"*May* 28.

...Towards evening, Turkish stragglers from the camp, and
others...flocked into the town, *and perpetrated the most atrocious crimes.* To pillage and wanton devastation, they added
violation and murder. The Tartars pointed out, as victims to

their cupidity and lust, those who had made themselves ob-
noxious to their ignorance and fanaticism...One miscreant was
shot as he came down the street in triumph, waving a sword
wet with the blood of a poor child whom he had hacked to
pieces"!!! [Reader, drop a tear for your country, by whose
means and assistance such atrocities are perpetrated. The
Hango massacre, revolting as it was, was nothing in infamy to
this.] "Others," continues the eye-witness, "were *slain in the
very act of committing horrible outrages.*" [What of their *souls,*
"Christian" warrior?] "Some were borne off, wounded, to the
prison or the hospital; and at last *respect for life was established
by its destruction*"!

But, as if congratulating the friends of Christianity and
humanity upon this 'consequence' of war, the writer adds,
"there was not, to be sure, a *general* massacre"; but, the
moral sense at last predominating, he admits that "even savages would have refrained from slaughtering the inhabitants
of a town which had submitted, and thrown itself upon their
mercy", although the Crimean heroes would not. French,
English, and Turks, are represented by this eye-witness—the
Times' special correspondent, who seemed to think that on the
whole he was describing a glorious event—as outvieing each
other in one of the vilest pillages and most atrocious scenes of
debauchery and bloodshed recorded in the darkest annals of
our history. No wonder that some poor heart-broken victim
should have been driven to inscribe on the panel of a smashed
door, leading into a building strewed with "broken urns, statues pounded to pieces, burnt bones, and vases containing dust
and ashes scattered on the floor", the following epitaph :—
"En entrant dans ce temple, où reposent les (souvenirs?)
d'un siècle passé, j'ai reconnu les traces d'une invasion des
Vandales. Hélas! Français ou Anglais, faites la guerre à la
(postérité), mais ne la faites pas à l'histoire. Si vous avez la
prétention d'être nations civilisées, ne faites pas la guerre des
barbares!'" "An admonition", says the correspondent, "which
was only too much needed, whoever were the perpetrators of
the ruin within". What a comment upon our country, our
associates, and our cause! "Frenchmen or Englishmen! wage
war with the present and the future, if you will, but respect the
dead. If you profess to be civilized nations, show yourselves
something better than savages"!!

And such seems to be our mission in the Crimea. How
much better the other towns we have taken have fared, remains to be told. "Yenikale", says the same correspondent,
"was set on fire in two places yesterday, and it required all the
exertions of the authorities to prevent the flames spreading and

devastating the whole place. The houses are smashed open, the furniture broken to pieces, and booty and plundering are the order—or the disorder—of the day."

"We *burnt* 16,000 sacks of oats, 360,000 sacks of corn, and 100,000 sacks of flour, and destroyed 300 merchant ships. At Berdiansk and Genitchi, 7,000,000 rations were destroyed." At Kertch the Russians destroyed "4,000,000 lbs. of corn and 500,000 lbs. of flour."

"Sir G. Brown intends to bring off the cattle."

Such is war, its principles, its incidents, and its religion!

"*Thou visitest the earth, and blessest it. Thou preparest corn. [Thou] bringest food out of the earth...and bread to strengthen man's heart.*" (Ps. civ.)

"*If ye love me, keep my commandments.*"

"*For the Son of Man shall come in the glory of His Father with his angels: and then He shall reward every man according to His work.*" (St. Matt. xvi, 27.)

Now, what think ye of these parallel columns? Do they both breathe the same spirit—both teach the same doctrine? Does "love your enemies" mean burn their buildings, destroy their food, sack their houses, ruin their families, starve and butcher their innocent children? Does "resist not evil" mean slaughter, bombard, sap, mine, and destroy? Does "do good to them that hate you" mean sink their ships, annihilate their commerce, plunder their towns, and render their country a desert? Can, then, anything more opposite to the spirit and genius of the Gospel be conceived than war? I trust you will now see the reason of my surprise at the request you made me yesterday—viz. to pray for success upon our arms. I know it has been said that what is meant by that, is praying for victory in order to bring about a permanent peace. But if war be an evil, which I think I have sufficiently shown,—and war without these 'incidents' cannot exist,—then, in conquering a peace, we are "*doing evil that good may come*"; and such peace, depend upon it, will neither be lasting nor salutary. Good bye.

Sol. Good bye: BLESSED ARE THE PEACE-MAKERS, FOR THEY SHALL BE CALLED THE CHILDREN OF GOD.

THE END.

T. RICHARDS, PRINTER, 37 GREAT QUEEN STREET.

HE CONDUCT OF THE WAR.

A SPEECH

DELIVERED IN

THE HOUSE OF COMMONS

ON TUESDAY, 12TH OF DECEMBER, 1854,

BY

IE RIGHT HON. SIDNEY HERBERT, M.P.,

&c. *&c.*

LONDON:
JOHN MURRAY, ALBEMARLE STREET.

1854.

LONDON : PRINTED BY WILLIAM CLOWES AND SONS, STAMFORD STREET,
AND CHARING CROSS.

A SPEECH,

&c.   &c.

Mr. S. Herbert rose and said,—Sir, the charges which have
been brought against the Government to-night are of a character
so serious that I hope the House will grant me their attention
while I endeavour to give an answer to the statements of the right
honourable gentleman the member for Droitwich, and to offer
that explanation of the course of the Government which he claimed
it as a right—and justly claimed it, as a member of Parliament—
to exact from them. That explanation I will endeavour to give
by a plain and straightforward narrative of the events in this war
as they occurred, so far as they came under the direction of the
Government; and the House of Commons must then judge
whether, when they have considered the past conduct of the
Government in the prosecution of the war, the Government are
entitled to ask for further powers and further assistance for the
purpose of carrying it out with vigour. Sir, the charges, as I
understand them, which have been made by the right honourable
baronet are many in number. He states that the army was originally sent out by the Government without any distinct plan or
intention; that when, at last, the Government resolved upon a
plan, it was not such a plan as was justifiable, considering the
forces at their command, and the information they possessed of the
power and strength of the enemy they were about to attack. The
right honourable gentleman says further, that the army was too
small for its object; that that army was not a well-appointed, but
an ill-appointed army; and he quoted instances in which it had
suffered in its efficiency from the want of due preparation on the
part of the Government. He says, also, that that army was sent

B 2

out too late; that the reinforcements were not sufficient; that that army, too weak in the first instance, was allowed, by the neglect at home, to dwindle down till it was absolutely insignificant. Now, I cannot do better than state—and I will do it in a very few sentences—what was the intention of the Government at the time that this army was first sent into the field; and I will show next what efforts were made in order to produce that army on the field in the highest state of discipline and efficiency; and thus you will see how much truth there is in the allegations that the army was too weak for its purpose, and that it was suffered to become still weaker by the want of reinforcements. Now, it was in April that the Government sent instructions to Lord Raglan as to the course he should pursue with the army under his orders. That army was numerically very inferior in strength to that now under his command.

Let me here say that in every step we took at home or abroad, through our minsters here, through our generals there, we acted in concert with our allies (hear, hear), whose good faith in council has been as signal as their gallantry in the field; and when I speak of instructions given or intentions entertained, I speak of intentions entertained and instructions given, not by the English Government alone, but by the allied Governments acting in strict concert together. Well, at the time this army was sent to occupy a portion of the Turkish territory, we had a large fleet in the Black Sea. There was then a very powerful Russian army occupying the Danubian Principalities. There had been but few contests then between the Turkish and the Russian forces, and the strength of the Russian army had not been broken by disease and the deficiency of their commissariat. Those who had the best means of forming a military opinion in this matter had not then very great confidence in the power of the Turkish army to resist the attacks which the Russians might direct against it, and thought—and, I believe, justly thought—that in the then aspect of affairs there was danger that a bold stroke might be made against the Turkish capital, and that the Bosphorus might fall into the hands of the Emperor of Russia. I am not now speaking of things that were probable, but in war you must also look to things that are possible, and guard against them. There was also the possibility that if the Turks failed to resist successfully the attacks on their position at Widdin and Kalafat, the Balkan might be turned, or that the Russians might, without crossing the Balkan range, go to the right of it, and advance down on Constantinople, and that the capital would in that way have been endangered.

Well, our army was occupied in ascertaining what would be the best line of defence, and strengthening it, in order to keep Constantinople safe from any *coup-de-main*. But Lord Raglan, in his instructions, was further told that a portion of our army should be encamped at Unkiar Skelessi, not only on account of the salubrious and well-watered nature of that portion of the country, but also because it placed him within reach of Varna, should the line of the Balkan be attempted to be forced by the Russians, and likewise because, if any attempt should have to be made on the Russian territory, such as was ultimately contemplated, great advantages would be enjoyed there for carrying out that object. I mention this to show that the Government had a distinct plan, which was—first, to secure the Dardanelles; next, to defend Constantinople; next, that capital being safe, to defend the lines of the Balkan; and, lastly, to be ready to attempt to strike a blow at some vital part of the Russian empire. That which had been foreseen took place: the Russians forced the Danube, Silistria was invested, and Omar Pasha considered that he was in great danger, and that he should be unable to maintain that fortress unless the allies made a combined advance that should threaten and menace the Russian army, and so force them to throw up the siege. We all recollect the events of that siege. We all recollect the gallantry of our own countrymen in a miserable outpost of that fortress (hear); but it was not their gallantry alone or their valour, but also a consciousness on the part of the Russians that an advance of the allies from Shumla and Varna rendered it impossible for them to maintain their position, that caused them to raise the siege.

We are apt after the fact to underrate the value of success achieved (hear, hear), and I have to-night heard a right honourable gentleman speak of gallant exploits elsewhere in a tone that I did not expect to have heard. Silistria was relieved. An argument may be advanced, as to whether the importance of such relief should have been allowed to interpose before other military operations. No doubt that interposition lost time, but you gained immensely by it; you gained for the Turkish army a great moral *prestige*, and destroyed that *prestige* which had so long throughout

Europe been attached to the Russian army. It was the first great enterprise of the Russian arms in this war, and it failed. Do not undervalue the importance of that at the outset of a contest. Well, that accomplished, it remained for the Government to decide on the next enterprise which would most tend to strike some effectual blow at the power of Russia in the Black Sea, and so place her neighbours in a state of tranquillity. On the 27th the siege of Silistria was raised, and on the 29th instructions were sent to Lord Raglan—who, from the first, had been desired to ascertain by every means in his power the amount of the Russian forces in the Crimea, and to ascertain how far, with the powers at the disposal of the allies, an attempt on Sebastopol would be successful. The officers who commanded those two armies were men of great military experience, and the Government reposed in them—one of whom is now no more—as it does now in the survivor and the successor of the other, unbounded confidence. (Cheers.) The right honourable baronet asks whether we gave them any positive instructions after we had received any positive information on which we could rely? If we had shown so little trust and confidence in those men who were selected to hold posts of such responsibility as the command of our armies, we being six weeks distant from the scene of action—if we had had so little confidence in them as to have told them, whether your information be favourable or not, you must wait until we have decided on it and weighed the grounds of your recommendation—then the allied Governments would not only, as the honourable baronet has said, have lost weeks, but months, and delayed so long that no expedition could have been attempted. Those officers took every means to ascertain the force of Russia in the Crimea. They held a council of war, and decided, and, as I think, rightly decided, that the attempt ought to be made. (Hear.) They knew the strength of their forces, and, from information, the strength of the forces they would be likely to meet; and Lord Raglan knew better than any man what accession to his forces he could count upon—for no man knows better what is or is not the military capacity of England. From the moment they had come to a decision, the allied commanders applied every energy of their minds to make preparations for that immense armament which conveyed our armies to the Crimea.

Right honourable gentlemen talk of the lateness of the expedition, and think nothing so simple as the embarkation of 50,000

men, and of carrying them across the sea and landing them, in
face of an hostile army, with boats built and prepared for the
landing of horses and siege guns. Right honourable gentlemen
talk of this as of landing at a pier in a time of profound peace.
(Hear, hear.) These preparations took much labour, and reflect
infinite credit cn those engaged in them, and I do not know that
any expedition ever sailed so perfect and complete in all its departments ; and, with the exception of that confusion which must
of necessity arise in moving so vast a body of men on so capri-
cious an element as the sea, I do not think that there was ever
moved so immense a force with so little loss and with so great
success. (Cheers.) Was the army landed in the Crimea so insufficient for the purpose for which it was intended ? Lord Raglan
took 27,000, which, together with our allies, formed a force of
more than 50,000 men. What had they to meet? Nearly the
whole of the Russian force in the Crimea, and they met it in an
entrenched position, which gave to their numbers an advantage
almost equivalent to doubling their force. They held on the
heights of Alma a position as strong as that which we held at
Inkermann, but they held it with a very different result. (Hear,
hear.)

Let me now ask whether there was nothing else that delayed
this expedition? Before it sailed from Varna there broke out a
fearful pestilence among our troops ; that pestilence thinned their
ranks most grievously, and our troops had to meet an enemy worse
than any human enemy and far more dispiriting and terrible to
the soldiers. We were, unfortunately, not the only sufferers ; our
allies suffered also from this disease, and among them its ravages
were more fearful than among our own troops. I do not exactly
know the extent of the loss they suffered, but I know the loss from
disease in both armies was far greater than any which we sustained in action. (Hear.) No sooner had that disease culminated,
and commenced to decline among the troops on land, than it broke
out in the fleet, which put to sea, as it was thought that the disease could so best be remedied ; but the fleet soon returned,
having in a few hours sustained a loss the mortality of which, from
its rapidity, was fearful. We left Lord Raglan and Marshal St.
Arnaud to recruit their army, and to raise them from that depres-
sion consequent on sickness, while making the preparations for the
invasion of the Crimea. But is it clear that, had they been able

to land in the Crimea earlier, they would have been able to have gained much as compared with the enemy? The difficulty which the Russians had to contend with in receiving reinforcements arose from the difficulty of passing over a soil which became broken up in wet weather. Therefore, the longer the fine weatner, the longer could the Russians pour in reinforcements; that they made good use of their time none could deny, and I suppose that there never was an army moved on land so skilfully and rapidly as was the corps of General Dannenberg which was brought from Odessa.

The right honourable baronet has said, that we have under-rated the power and skill of our enemy. I recollect that last session I made some observations on that head; and I said that the public opinion of the country was doing that which the right honourable baronet now accuses us of doing. From the campaign on the Danube, which had this peculiarity, that there was not one pitched battle fought during it, the public chose to assume that the Russian power was waning, if not extinct, and that there was nothing easier than to conquer wherever we chose. I pointed out that the Russian soldier, who is a Russian peasant, is a man of a primitive nature, and, like all primitive people, is strongly and ardently attached to his native country. We are apt to think that those of a country which has no free institutions like our own are unable to feel that patriotism which we feel; but we have had a lesson in this respect, and others will admit, now that they have seen the defence made of Sebastopol, the tenacity with which the Russians defend their country, a tenacity to which when I for-merly alluded I was accused of connivance. (Hear.) But the right honourable baronet states, that the army was insufficient in number, and has been utterly without reinforcements. The army, when first sent out, was composed of four divisions, the 1st, 2nd, 3rd, and Light Division, besides cavalry and artillery. In June, before the orders were given to make a descent on the Crimea, if circumstances were such as to justify such an attack, a fifth divi-sion was formed and placed under the command of the lamented Sir G. Cathcart. Now let me state the reinforcements that were sent out to the army:—in June there were sent 941 men; in July, 4588 men; in August, 2032 men—yet we are told that from the moment that the expedition was decided on no reinforcements were sent to the army.

Sir J. PAKINGTON.—I did not say that.

Then I was so unfortunate as to have misunderstood the right honourable baronet; but, perhaps he will admit that, subsequent to the orders, and subsequent to the landing in the Crimea, he said no attempt was made to reinforce the army. Now let us see how that stands. In September there were 1286 men sent out; in October, 2855; in November, 7037. (Hear.) Now these were before other reinforcements, which I admit were called for by subsequent events, and which were requested by Lord Raglan; but I do not count them, or seek to take any advantage from them, but month by month state to you the troops sent out. But you may argue that these reinforcements were small for a power like England, that can pour out its battalions like water. But, I ask, on whom rests the responsibility that England, at the commencement of a war, must make small wars. Why is it? It is because through every Government and every Parliament, we have always had the same stereotyped system of economy in military affairs.

I am speaking the whole plain truth in this matter. (Hear.) I am as much to blame as any one. I have held for some years the responsible situation of Secretary of War, and I know what have been my own short-comings in this respect, but this too I know, that whenever I have brought forward, as I have done, what are called peace estimates, I have constantly been met with motions for large reductions. I say, therefore, that it has been the fault of all parties, all administrations, every Parliament; I am afraid I cannot give my assent to any exception, however eager I may be to do so; I have seen administrations formed of various parties—I have seen them taking different courses on almost every conceivable subject, but on one they have agreed, and that has been the one to which I have alluded—one of improvident economy. What has been the result?

At the commencement of the war we had to make means, and to create an army, and to use it at the same time. I recollect at the time when the Militia Bill was brought forward by the honourable member for Midhurst—and every year that has passed has confirmed the opinion I entertained of the wisdom of that measure—we had a great many discussions on the military available strength of the country, and honourable gentlemen used arguments to show that after deducting the troops necessary for the occupation of our garrisons, we had not 10,000 available bayonets left in England.

Well, now I have shown the number of men originally sent out, and of the reinforcements since sent; I will now add to them those that have been ordered to embark from the different Mediterranean garrisons, and which are sent from home, including also 1700 men waiting for ships. I am not now speaking of what have been actually under Lord Raglan's command, but of those which are passing under his command—which, when they have passed there will from first to last have been, in cavalry, infantry, artillery, and sappers, 53,044 men. This is the number of non-commissioned officers and privates, exclusive of officers. If you add them, the numbers will be between 54,000 and 55,000 men. (Hear, hear.) I do not believe that the country is aware of the efforts that have been made—they have seen it stereotyped through leading articles that Lord Raglan has been left with 16,000 bayonets. But what does 16,000 bayonets mean? It means all that are left, after deducting all the men on detachment duty, all the cavalry, all the artillery, all the engineers, and all officers and non-commissioned officers, and the 16,000 bayonets are put forward as the whole available army. Why, the Duke of Wellington had at the battle of Waterloo only 18,000 British bayonets, and if you will subtract all the officers, non-commissioned officers, cavalry, and artillery, and men not actually engaged, you will attain your object in making a small show upon paper, but you will deceive yourselves and the country as to the efforts she is putting forth. (Hear, hear.)

The right honourable baronet has said, and with perfect fairness and truth, that the Government has no right to complain of the House of Commons, and they have behaved with fairness and liberality, and have not made objections to any call or demand which the Government has made; but the right honourable gentleman says, that the question is, whether these powers or further powers should be intrusted to the hands of those who have shown so little wisdom, prudence, and foresight? The right honourable baronet drew a picture of a Member of Parliament's duty: it was his duty to give his support to a war which he felt to be just, and to give his support also to a Government he thought capable of conducting it efficiently. He says, however, that he gave extraordinary powers to the present Government, whom he thought incapable of using them with wisdom, prudence, or foresight. If that be his rule, it is not mine. If we are to derive any advantage from this strange proceeding on his part, I reject it; if he thinks the Government incapable of carrying on affairs, it is not his duty to intrust them with power, but to transfer it to some other men more honest and capable of conducting affairs, so as to satisfy himself and the country.

The right honourable baronet has also asserted that they had neglected to supply the army with proper appointments; he founds his charge on a proceeding which, in a military point of view, was necessary, and on which the government could not have dictated, and neither did they pretend to dictate, to military men. The right honourable baronet says they landed without tents, and he conceives that the executive were in fault for having sent out a great army without a sufficiency of tents; but every regiment that went out with its arms and munition took also tents, and I do not believe that any army ever before went out so perfectly appointed in these respects. There is no doubt about their having the tents, but it is said Lord Raglan landed on the 16th of September without tents. The night was wet, and the men were exposed to a great deal of suffering, and they did for a few days that which the Duke of Wellington and the Spanish army did for four years. No doubt much sickness was caused by this—it is very easy to judge of this after the fact—and Lord Raglan is blamed for having landed without tents, and having brought them so unprovided to Balaklava.

But let me put another question, and let any one judge whether Lord Raglan is to be blamed. He knew that they had to meet a very powerful army, which had intrenched itself, and it was very obvious that within a short time of landing, and probably at the time of landing, they would have to meet an energetic, determined, and skilful enemy. Lord Raglan might have brought all his tents, but then he would have left behind him all those battalions the space for which would have been taken up by the tents. A powerful force is stationed at the Alma, and nothing can be done until their position is forced or turned. Now, if the result of the battle of the Alma, instead of being a glorious victory, had been an undecided success in consequence of the want of two or three battalions, the expedition would have been lost, and what would then have been said of Lord Raglan? (Hear, hear.) It would have been said, "Why did you fill your ships with ambulances and tents when you had men, and such men, lying idle at

Varna? You were going upon an expedition in which you knew that the first blow was everything, and to take men with you, and plenty of them, should have been the one and the only consideration." But now the battle of the Alma has been won it is easy for the right honourable gentleman to say that it might have been won with fewer men. Just so. The right honourable gentleman thinks nothing of the expedition to Bomarsund. There was, certainly, he says, a blockade, but you sent your great ships into the Baltic upon an expedition ending in nothing. One right honourable baronet thinks nothing of the capture of islands almost inaccessible, held by a very powerful enemy, in which buildings had been marked out for erection which would have made them into another Cronstadt, or another Helsingfors, so that there might be in the Gulf of Finland another perpetual menace to another capital. This is the result which the right honourable gentleman treats with such supreme contempt; but the Emperor of the French differs from him in opinion, for he gave a marshal's bâton to the general who commanded the French troops engaged in the expedition. (Hear, hear.)

I now come back to the Alma, and the right honourable gentleman's charge, that tents were not provided for the troops. I hope the explanation I have given will be obvious to every one and satisfactory to the country. I do not believe that one iota of blame attaches to Lord Raglan for that proceeding. (Cheers from the Opposition.) I believe he did what every man in his place ought to do—he judged of the circumstances as they then stood, he did not pretend to prophesy the success of the army, but he took every means to insure it. It is now easy to say that his success was certain, and that he should have left men behind and taken tents with him instead.

I must here diverge for a moment to meet a charge which the right honourable gentleman has not made, but which has been frequently made elsewhere, and I shall make a very frank statement on that subject to the House; nor shall I, in defending what appears to me to be defensible, condescend for one moment to conceal what I think with respect to details which have been, in my opinion, unsatisfactory. Last session we had a great deal of discussion as to the merits of the commissariat, and the commissariat was then subjected to much popular criticism. I believe that the opinions then formed with regard to the commissariat were exaggerated, and not founded on fact, but I am not prepared to say that at the end of a long peace the commissariat, or any other department of the army, was necessarily, or could be, in as perfect a state as experience and practice could make it. I have no doubt, therefore, that there was ground for a certain portion of criticism upon the part of those who were determined to find fault; but the commissariat has outlived these criticisms, and I believe it is now universally admitted that there never was an army better fed than the army of Lord Raglan. Their rations have been increased, and they are now 50 per cent. larger in meat than the rations of British troops have been at any previous time. When fears arose as to their health from the non-use of vegetables, immediate steps were taken to supply them from Trieste, Venice, and Smyrna, with fresh vegetables; and when I heard that they were being sold to the men, I wrote to Lord Raglan, that, in my opinion, whatever was necessary to make the soldiers efficient in the peculiar position in which they were placed, with a view to the public service, ought to be supplied at the expense of the public. (Hear, hear.)

But it has been stated that there has been great mismanagement with respect to the medical department of the army during the campaign, and I am very anxious that the House should know the exact truth upon this subject, because, I think, nothing can be so detrimental to the public service as for the public to imagine that when our bravest men were laid prostrate by suffering, be it from wounds or be it from sickness, they met with heartless neglect at a time when they had earned for themselves a right to the utmost care and solicitude. Let me first state what was the amount of the staff which we sent out. For a long period no army had left the shores of England so large and so well appointed; and certainly none had ever left it to conduct operations so important, but so hazardous, as the army of Lord Raglan. It was felt that going to a climate so doubtful, the efficiency of the medical staff was a matter of paramount importance. When, therefore, the army was first organized, the Government took the opinion of a gentleman upon a matter of detail, which I instance in order to show the care and attention with which these matters were looked to: they took the opinion of a very eminent man, namely, Mr. Guthrie, a surgeon of great experience as well as talent, who had stated that there was an error in the organization of the medical department. He said, " You have but three medical officers to a regiment ; you have a large staff ; the staff-surgeon has none of that local interest in a regiment which the regimental surgeon has. In the field the regimental surgeon has the strongest interest in bringing his men to a state of health as rapidly as possible, and getting them back to their battalions, while the staff-surgeon has no interest, one way or the other, in clearing the hospitals ; and therefore do not give so many men to your staff, but give a fourth surgeon to every regiment, and your medical department will be more efficient."

Dr. Andrew Smith, the head of the medical department of the army, differed from Dr. Guthrie in this respect. He said, in no battle is every regiment engaged ; and, if you give a fourth surgeon to every regiment, those regiments which have suffered most will not have enough, while those who have not suffered at all will have too many. Those who have suffered must depend on the staff ; but the staff will be weakened, and the colonels of the regiments which have not been engaged will not let a surgeon of their own go, for they will say that their own regiments may be engaged on the next day. I consulted Lord Raglan as to which system he preferred, and he said he thought Dr. Guthrie was right. But there was great authority on either side ; and we therefore said to the one, " Take your large regimental establishment ;" and to the other, " Take your large staff establishment." (Hear, hear.) Dr. Andrew Smith had devoted himself to the work night and day ; he collected all the purveyors of hospitals who had had experience in previous wars. They met at his house, and drew up a report as to the proper amount of stores to be sent out. In this report they drew upon their recollections of the Peninsula, and made their calculations at so much per head. Well, we trebled it. The Government felt that since the period of the Peninsular war great improvements had been made, the comforts of the soldiers were now more attended to, and more must be done than had been done in the campaigns of Wellington. I mention this to show that it was our object to make these preparations for the army as good and as ample as possible. I am not saying that all has been done successfully, or could not have been done better, but that we spared no exertion to make it as efficient as we could. Now, how many gentlemen were appointed to the army ? Of staff medical officers there were 280, of regimental medical officers 192, and of

ordnance medical officers 14 ; making a total of 486, or, with the
nine medical officers of the 5th division, of 495. But upwards of
100 of these have been added since the battle of the Alma; but
at that time, also, it must be recollected that the force was much
smaller. At that battle the medical establishment, as it was at
first fixed for the army, amounted to 275. On looking at the
' Moniteur de l'Armée,' I find that the medical establishment for
the French army amounted to exactly the same number, 270 odd,
although their army was numerically larger than ours. If we had
chosen to limit our medical staff to the number engaged in the
Peninsula, we should have sent out one surgeon to every 145 men,
while the number we have sent is one to every 77 men.

Much complaint has been made upon this subject; and a great
deal of the blame which has been cast upon it is just in this sense,
that when sickness makes its ravages upon an army which is at
the same time engaged in constant operations against an enemy,
the strain upon the medical officers becomes so great that no number you can send will be sufficient. But was there no difficulty in
getting together this large staff? It was necessary to send all the
most experienced men we could find, and we drew from the depôts
all the regimental surgeons of military experience to send out ;
but it was also necessary to keep some at home, because we had
the cholera in England as well as in Turkey, and we could not
trust entirely to civilians for attendance upon the troops, because,
when such a case as the cholera arises, a civilian, who has a large
practice in the country, and whose clients are very important to him,
says, It will not be honest in me to receive your pay, as I can no
longer attend to your regiment. We had great difficulty in getting
these men together, for they were scattered about in emigrant
ships, in merchant ships, and in various other vocations in different
parts of the world. We also employed numbers of civilians, giving
them a temporary rank in the army ; and they did not wish for
more, as they were only desirous of the opportunity of getting
practice and experience.

I think the House will do me the justice to admit that, as far
as the medical staff is concerned, the Government cannot be
charged with looking at it in a niggard spirit, or with not antici-
pating great drains upon that establishment, which was just double
in number that which had ever before been sent with an English
army. I must not read to the House the long lists which have

been published of the *materiel* which was sent out. I am not speaking to that which is the weak point in the department—viz., its distribution, but to the fact of its having been prepared and sent out—to the fact that Dr. A. Smith was indefatigable in his endeavours to supply the army with every possible comfort, nay, with every possible luxury that could be of use in a hospital. The list contains the items of blankets and bedding, of cotton sheets 19,000, and everything upon that sort of scale. I will not take up time by reading it, but I wish to impress upon the House and upon the right honourable gentleman that it has not arisen from heartless indifference to the sufferings of the troops that they have been exposed to privations. (Hear, hear.)

I have alluded to a statement that after the battle of the Alma a great deal of unnecessary suffering was inflicted on our troops in consequence of the bad arrangements of the medical staff. I can refer upon this subject to documentary evidence, but I think I can put the case to the House in a manner which will convince them that there has been great misapprehension and great exaggeration of the evils which have existed, and which at the commencement of a war must exist. It was stated that the wounded of the British army at Alma lay upon the field of battle untended for two or three days—that they were brought down to the ships with their wounds undressed, and put on board one of them in such numbers that it was rendered unsafe. I believe that a great deal of this misapprehension arose from ignorance of what happened in places beyond the observation of those who made the allegations.

The French army took fewer men than we did, and carried their ambulances with them; they had, I rejoice to say, fewer wounded than we had, and, being nearer to the sea, all their wounded were carried immediately to the ships. Our troops were some of them four or five miles from the sea, and a field hospital was established at some farm-buildings at or near the spot where they had fallen. All the men whose cases permitted them to be moved were moved into it, and those who could not be moved were treated on the field, their wounds were dressed, and as much comfort afforded them as possible—little enough that is. All such plans after a great battle, and upon the battlefield, are necessarily rough and inefficient for the comfort of the men; but this is one of the stern necessities of war. The men were brought down the next day, or the day following, from the field-hospital, or from the field, and placed on board ship. It was supposed that those who were thus carried down were being brought for the first time from the spot at which they were wounded, and that no treatment had yet been afforded them; but I have evidence which satisfies me that in not one single instance was a man allowed to leave this field-hospital without his hurts being dressed. But I will take a previous case, namely that of the Kangaroo, after the landing at Old Fort; but it is quite true that a number of men, far beyond what she could possibly carry, were in the first instance placed on board the Kangaroo. The statement, however, that 1500 persons were placed on board is an exaggeration, for I believe that the number did not much, if at all, exceed 700. It was stated that the officer in command made a signal that he was overloaded, and that the medical officer remonstrated against so large a number being placed on board, and 450 only were sent in her. The medical department was free from blame; but persons commanding transports, and those who are without the same responsibility as medical men, are often very unwilling to put themselves out of the way for a department which is not their own. Some of the wounded were removed from the Kangaroo to another vessel. It was stated that hundreds died of the cholera during the passage; the number, I believe, was really 22, and that is a small proportion, when it is recollected there were many cholera cases, and that at that very period the proportion of deaths to sickness was greater than that here in the London hospitals. There was great confusion, great discomfort; but I maintain that these things cannot always be avoided in war. (Hear, hear.) In the position in which we were placed after the battle of the Alma the men could not be left on the field: Lord Raglan was obliged to remain two or three days on the spot because he was aware that if he left them they would be massacred by the Cossacks, and, of course, their sufferings on board ship were great before they reached the general hospital of Constantinople. But it is said that their wounds were not dressed during the whole time that they were on board ship. I am informed by surgeons accustomed to the treatment of gunshot wounds, that no surgeon would think of re-dressing a wound of this description within three or four days after it had been made; the great object being not to disturb the wound, and to keep the dressings wet. It may, therefore, be true, that the wounds were not dressed on board, and yet that the sufferers did not experience any unnecessary neglect.

I have dilated rather at length upon this subject because I do feel that, if it were true that anything like systematic or heartless indifference had been manifested by any department, but above all by the medical department, it would produce a terrible reaction in the spirit of the people of this country, and destroy that confidence in the administration and management of the army, which has of late years made it so much more easy to recruit its ranks.

As I am upon this point I may say a few words with regard to the general hospital at Scutari, and this is a subject which, I admit, has caused me much anxiety. The distance at which we are placed from the scene of action is such that we are helpless to assist in any great emergency; we can send out stores and men, but we cannot direct their immediate application. I will not conceal what I consider to be the real truth with regard to this hospital, although I have seen evidence upon both sides so contradictory that I would defy any man who was willing to give credit to either party to know what conclusion to come to. We have been told that it was not possible to procure lint in the hospital, and the greatest indignation has been expressed against the persons charged with these matters for leaving the hospital so unprovided. I have accounts from medical men, which I will not read. They are the persons who have been impugned, and unjustly impugned, by public opinion, and their statement is that there never was for a moment a deficiency in the stores, but there had been the greatest mismanagement as to their distribution—whether of lint, of linen, or of anything else. At the time the army left Varna the general hospital was there, and orders were then given that the stores should be sent down to Scutari, but that order, in the hurry and bustle of the departure, was never executed. The principal portion of the stores remained at Varna, while the whole mass of the wounded were sent to Scutari; fortunately there was with the assistance of the Turkish Government a sufficiency to meet the difficulty of the moment. A deficiency being apprehended, the medical officers accepted a loan of them from the Turkish Government for the use of the hospital. Therefore there was at one time an apprehended deficiency: there never was a positive deficiency: but I will tell you what there has been—there has been a system engendered during the peace which has greatly encumbered the hospitals; of check and counter-check for the purpose of economy. There have been all manner of forms to be gone through before stores could be issued to the medical officers. Every account I get says this; the medical men in their vocation are beyond all praise, especially those at the head of the establishment; they work night and day—their tenderness to the sick, their humanity, their zeal, their energy are mentioned by every one, friend and foe. But the deficiency is this: that, with plenty of stores, no one seemed to know where to lay their hands upon them: with plenty of materials at their disposal, the forms were so cumbrous that they never could be produced with that rapidity which was necessary for the purposes of a military hospital. The moment we heard complaints of this kind we sent out a commission with authority to inquire into the causes of these evils and set them right. We thought there might be timidity on the part of some of the officials in asking for what they might require, and we telegraphed to Lord Stratford, telling him the supplies were to be unlimited, and that the hospital was to be provided with everything. Private benevolence came in aid. We did everything we could, and I am glad to see, by the accounts I get from persons on whose judgment I can depend, that things have been in some degree set right. One gentleman, whose letter is private, but whose name alone would be a guarantee that he was not disposed to criticise too favourably upon this subject, says, "I see there much to blame and much to praise. But day by day I see manifest improvement. To manage more than 3000 casualties of the worst nature is indeed a task to be met in an entirely satisfactory way by nothing short of a miraculous energy." He says, "With regard to the past, I could pick many a hole, and show where head has been wanted and duty neglected: but I see so much exertion being made that I will throw a veil over that; if the wheel is in the rut, at any rate I can say every one is putting his shoulder to the wheel to get it out again." I do believe that those who have been so free to blame have not really considered and made allowance for the difficulties of the case. When 1000 or 1100 wounded men are simultaneously brought into a hospital, if you had all the order and all the appliances you could wish, you never could prevent a scene of confusion arising from the sudden influx of so many wounded men. (Cheers.)

I hope the House will do me the justice to acknowledge that in speaking on this question I have not concealed my honest opinion. (Hear, hear.) I might have read to you flat contradictions of everything that has been advanced, written by men who made their statements in perfect good faith, who could give the dates of the particular cases with the greatest accuracy; and I have no doubt they would give to the House the exact facts as to particular accusations, but they would not give to the House what I should like it to have—a fair general view of the real circumstances of the case. If I might be allowed to say one word on this subject before I leave it, it is this:—One thing which the Government did to insure the comfort of the sick and wounded has been eminently successful. The House will recollect that, some time ago, a lady undertook to carry out a number of nurses for the purpose of alleviating the sufferings of the sick and wounded. I have received not only from medical men, but from many others who have had an opportunity of making observations, letters couched in the highest possible terms of praise. I will not repeat the words, but no higher words of praise could be applied to women for the wonderful energy, the wonderful tact, the wonderful tenderness, combined with the extraordinary courage and self-devotion which have been displayed by that lady (loud cheers); and I am glad to say that the characteristics which have been shown by that lady, the force and influence of her character, seem to have penetrated all those working with her, and I believe not only the patients themselves, but every person connected with the hospital, will be benefited by the admixture of this new element in the management of a military hospital. (Cheers.)

I have been led away from my subject in this digression, but I hope the House will pardon me, and I will now come back to what I was saying in answer to the observations of the right honourable baronet. I have stated what was the force of our armament—I have shown the amount of the army which was originally sent, and which is now about to be sent to Lord Raglan, taking the reinforcements due to him, and adding them to those already in his possession; and a letter has been put into my hand from Sir H. Ward, stating—and I was delighted to hear it—that he had letters from Admiral Boxer, in which he mentioned that 24,000 English and French troops had passed through the Bosphorus since the 5th of last month. I have shown you the number of the reinforcements, I have shown you that they amounted first, in June, to 941; July, to 4580; August, 2032; September, 1286; October, 2855; and November, 7037, making altogether 18,739, exclusive of the reinforcements since sent; and I have shown you, including the original army and the other reinforcements, we have sent out over 54,000 men; and I ask you whether, consulting our history, England, in the first year of any war in which she was engaged, ever sent forth such an army as this. (Cheers.)

You say, and say with truth—and I believe you—" You have absorbed our reserve." We have done so. The right honourable baronet says the questions he put to-night were not all, and that on another day he might call us to account, and ask us why we sent an expedition against Sebastopol at all. I will not wait for that time, but I will tell him why. Because we knew that Sebastopol is the stronghold of the power of Russia in the south (cheers); we knew that the blockade of Russia, however effectual, will not strike home in a manner that will be sensibly felt; and we knew that the destruction of her fortresses along the Circassian coast, although it shakes her power to the centre in those provinces of Asia which she has of late years appropriated, is not still such a blow as would be inflicted if by any means at our disposal we could destroy her fleet and arsenal at Sebastopol. It was a great undertaking; I admit it was a great hazard, but I tell you next year it would have been impossible. Round that mighty fortress, day by day, and night by night, have been rising chains of forts; and, if we give them time, they will continue to rise until it is absolutely impregnable. If Sebastopol is not taken or destroyed in this campaign, it will never be taken or destroyed. There was a great risk in the undertaking, it is said. I say there was. But I recollect a friend of mine, last session, saying he had seen a gentleman of influence in the City, who had told him there was but one feeling there of unanimity as to the way in which the war should be carried on. He said, " We all hope that the war will be carried on with the utmost vigour and determination, but no risks must be run, and no danger of disaster incurred." (Laughter.) Now, if we can conduct a war with that happy mixture of energy and determination, combined with no risk to ourselves—that happy mixture of prudence and boldness which would inflict all the loss upon the enemy and none upon ourselves—truly we might say the golden age of war has come. (Hear, hear.) But in carrying on war you must run great risks if you acquire great advantages. (Cheers.)

It is said it was a great hazard. Unquestionably it was; and I know that many military men thought it too great a hazard to be attempted; but others equal in authority said, and said truly, " You must do it now, or you never will do it at all." I admit that there was very great hazard, but, at the same time, the prize was of such enormous importance that we should have been unworthy of our places if we had not attempted, while we could with any chance of success, to strike a blow at the only vulnerable place, which is the very centre and heart of the power of Russia in the Black Sea. (Cheers.)

Well, I hope that the right honourable baronet will be satisfied with this answer, which is the only one I can give him. We know the hazards of war; but it is easy to judge of events after they have taken place. (Ministerial cheers.) But let the right honourable baronet reflect on the course which was taken by certain parties with reference to this subject during the last session. I confess that all last summer, when I heard the language in which the Government was urged to make an attempt upon Sebastopol — they thought the subject had escaped the attention of the Government, I suppose—but the language in which it was urged was in itself so arrogant, so ignorant, and so presumptuous, that I used to feel, when I heard it, a sort of superstitious fear that such arrogance and such presumption would bring down a judgment from Heaven upon us. They talked of Russian power—judging from the weakened, dispirited, and demoralized army that could make no progress in the campaign upon the Danube—they talked of the power of Russia as if it were nothing. We did not enter into this war in that spirit. We knew the great resources she possessed, and we did everything in our power to ensure success. It is true that I have heard a criticism made by some military men upon the whole proceeding. They say,—you have sent out more men than you can well maintain, you have sent out what you will find it difficult to feed: it is much more than you can manage. That was the difficulty I spoke of before—of making a great start in the first year of the war. It is a difficulty which you have to encounter when you have to make an army at the same time that you are to use it. Recollect this—we have few well-seasoned soldiers in this country.

See the difficulties we have had to encounter. We have no conscription in England : we have no compulsory service whatever

in England, except for internal defence ; we have to trust entirely
to the voluntary. system. You cannot make an army as other
nations may. You cannot make an army by a stroke of the pen,
or by an ukase raise 100,000 soldiers. We must get men willing
to come ; but on the other hand, when they do come, you have got
the materials which no conscription in the world can furnish
(cheers)—you have got for your materials men not dragged from
their reluctant homes against their wills, and from their peaceful
pursuits, to be forced into scenes of blood and scenes of horror to
which they were averse. You have got free men—men animated
by high spirit, full of adventure, full of life, full of ambition—men
whom no suffering can break, who can never complain that one
hardship or suffering to which they have been exposed has been
forced upon them by a tyrannical Government. You have had
that difficulty, but you have had another—at least when we are
talking of augmentation, we have had a difficulty which has pressed
very much upon us; for some time emigration to a great extent
has been going on from this country, and more especially from the
sister country, Ireland, where it has dried up the sources of our
military supply. You have had great prosperity in trade and
agriculture, and consequent demand for labour, and all that would
not be in favour of the recruiting serjeant. But when I look back
to the records of history, and see what were the means by which
in former wars we attempted to get men—how we persuaded men
into the militia by a bounty of ten guineas, and drafted them out
of it by a bounty of eleven guineas, and, after all, we could only
raise 24,000 men in one year—and when I look at what has been
done during this the first year of the war, I must confess the contrast is not unfavourable. (Cheers.) Taking into account the
enlistments, both in the regulars and the East India Company's
service, and the Marines, we should have added by free enlistment
something like 40,000 men, such as I have described, to our forces.
I do say, then, I reply with confidence to the inquiry as to the
augmentation of the army. We are getting men not faster than
they are required, but faster than we can form them into regiments,
drill them, and make them skilful and useful soldiers of their
Queen and country. (Cheers.)

And here on that point I will stop to say that Lord Hardinge,
the Commander-in-Chief, at the very commencement issued a
regulation in regard to the troops for the East, that he would not

allow a single man to go out unless he was previously practised in the use of the Minié rifle. It has been the fashion for some to depreciate the value of the services of Lord Hardinge. I have served with Lord Hardinge as Commander-in-Chief, and with others as Commander-in-Chief, and I have been able to see what Lord Hardinge has been able to accomplish under circumstances of great difficulty. If you look at the nature of the successes which our arms have achieved in the Crimea, I think it will strike you that the next thing to be noticed, after the indomitable courage and fortitude of the men, is the skill with which they have used their weapons, and the superiority of the weapons which have been placed in their hands. If it had not been for Lord Hardinge, I do not believe you would have had a division armed with Minié rifles. I do not mean that Lord Hardinge introduced them ; but if he had not during the short time he was at the head of the Ordnance Department imparted a great impulse to their intro-duction, they would not have been in the use they are now. Many officers of high military rank were notoriously prejudiced in favour of the old regulation musket, and could not be got out of the routine ; and even such men as Sir C. Napier, enlightened and intelligent as he was, clung to the last to Brown Bess, and said, " For God's sake don't take away Brown Bess." But Lord Hardinge had made a regulation that not a recruit should leave this country unless he was properly instructed in the skilful use of this formidable arm. And what is the opinion of the men as to the use of the rifle ? and what was the opinion of those not armed with it, from witnessing its effect ? That opinion was manifested on the dreadful day of Inkermann, where, whenever a man, not having the rifle, saw a man fall who had, he ran, seized his Minié, and used it for the rest of the day. It is not only the superiority of the weapon, but the consciousness which it gives the man who has it that he is dependent upon his skill, and must devote his mind to exercise that skill. The result is that, instead of firing at random, and only one ball in 600 or 700 taking effect, they saw the soldier using his weapon with the facility with which a gamekeeper would his fowlingpiece, and taking the proper pre-caution to make every shot tell.

Well, we have had this army to create, to drill, and to send out. Men are coming in rapidly ; we shall be able to augment the re-giments largely, and thus establish a reserve, so that another year it shall not be said, as it has been this year, "You have put our all upon one great effort." It has been said, we should have sent out earlier two, three, four, five, or six regiments; but could we have done so? What will the right honourable baronet say when he is told how long it takes to make a soldier? What were the regiments that have been sent out? Three months ago regiments that have been sent out were in our colonies, or returning from a tropical climate, mere skeletons of regiments. They were to be engaged in Crimean duty, and had to be totally reformed. Some of these regiments were not in England at this time; some were in Canada; others in the West Indies. How, then, can it be said to us, reinforcements should have been sent out three months ago? We could not get a man of those regiments which the right honourable baronet says ought to have been sent out; and he must recollect that we cannot create an army by a stroke of a pen; we must get the men first, then make them into soldiers by drilling them, and instructing them in the skilful use of their weapon; for nothing will be so injurious to the reputation of our army as sending men into the field inefficient for their duty. (Cheers.)

I hope, Sir, that this House will believe that the Government have not been neglectful of these considerations, and have made every exertion to raise and strengthen our army. Look back at the history of all previous expeditions, at the commencement of our wars, and show me one which has been equal in strength to that which has now been sent out. Show me one in which at the end of the first campaign they had come out with a higher reputation. Can it be said now, as Sir Henry Bunbury says of our army before the expedition to Egypt, that the public had lost all confidence in the skill, and even the courage, of our officers and men; and that one of the greatest benefits of the successful campaign of Sir R. Abercrombie was to restore the reputation of the armies after the disastrous disgraces which England had undergone.

But I want to know what is our position at present. I want to know whether, at any period in the history of England, our military character stands higher than it does at this moment. I want to know what is the effect upon the public opinion of Europe of the manner in which our battalions have conducted themselves. I want to know what is the effect upon Russia, and upon its armies, of the manner in which our battalions have repulsed every attack they have made upon them. Sir, I must say I think that those persons who take upon themselves to criticise our operations, and to say that Alma ought to have been turned instead of stormed, could not have studied the map of the country on which their opinions are offered, or they would see that the ground on the right of the Russians on that occasion was so steep and so inaccessible that its commander did not even think it necessary to strengthen it: and if Lord Raglan, whose conduct has been attacked, and whose reputation has been assailed, for not turning that position, had adopted the course which has been so suggested, he could have done nothing which the commander of the Russian troops could have more desired. He would have desired nothing better than to have separated the English and French armies, and to have placed his own army between the English forces and the ships, which formed the basis of our operations.

So, likewise, it has been alleged against Lord Raglan that he ought to have assaulted Sebastopol immediately after the march to Balaklava. But, Sir, I don't think that we, sittin here, are very good judges of such operations. (Cheers.) I know that many eminent military men on the spot, and knowing the circumstances, thought otherwise, and were highly averse to such an undertaking. Talk of leading flesh and blood against batteries, and that that ought not to be risked, and that positions should be turned! What would such men have said if he had led the troops against a town of which we knew nothing of the interior, where it was impossible to say how much of Prince Menschikoff's army might have been, of the defence of which we knew nothing, and where our soldiers might have been exposed to massacre in detail in a town every house of which was a fortification? I confess I do defer to the opinions of the eminent men who commanded the French and English armies on that occasion. (Cheers.)

But the right honourable baronet says the troops have been exposed to unnecessary privations. Now, is it true, as has been asserted by the right honourable baronet, that we took no precautions with regard to warm clothing? Warm clothing was sent out; and that brings me to another point. It has been, as we all know, a matter of great regret that the ship conveying those stores was unfortunately lost. But I must say that that loss has been greatly exaggerated. The value of the cargo of that ship was estimated at no less a sum than 500,000*l.*; but I understand that it was not more than 180,000*l.* This was, no doubt, a great loss. But immediate steps were taken to remedy that loss; supplies were obtained from Constantinople, and there is reason to hope that that loss has not been felt. With regard to the clothing of the army, it so happened that when Lord Raglan applied for clothing the answer was, "It has been already ordered, and a great part has been already embarked." So that the letters of Lord Raglan in asking for supplies had been already anticipated.

Then the Government have been charged with being ignorant of the severity of the climate of the Crimea, and with not adopting those means which are best calculated to protect the troops from its injurious influence. Now, what is the position in which we have been placed? I have a letter from a gentleman, a member of this House, but whom I do not now see in his place, but a gentleman whose opinion is always worth having, who says—"*Experto crede*, I know the climate of the Crimea well; don't believe the accounts that are published about the temperature; but whatever you do, follow the custom of the country; they must know best, and they clothe themselves in skins and not in woollen." I then requested the opinion of a person of great experience in Arctic researches, and he came to me and said, "Don't dress the men in skins, stick to wool, that is the only thing to keep them warm." (Laughter.) I ask the House how was I to decide between these two authorities? Without attempting to do so, I thought the safest thing was to take the advice of both, and to send out both skins and woollen (cheers); and my hope is, that before long every man in the army will have a change, both of woollen and of skins, from top to toe. We have sent out seal-skin caps, which are so made as to cover the face and ears; waterproof leggings also are supplied; likewise an outer coat of waterproof, under which can be worn a long vest made of tweed lined with hare-skin, rabbit-skin, cat-skin, and every other kind of skin. (Hear, and laughter.) Besides this, we have sent out a peculiar description of coat —not lined in the usual style, but according to what is called the Canada fashion; and lastly, there will be a sheep-skin coat, I hope, for each man. Thus, I think it will be seen that the men will be supplied with ample means to clothe themselves both with skins and woollens that must keep them warm. (Hear, hear.)

Then with regard to providing huts for the troops, what have the Government done? They felt that, in this particular, time was everything. To have them built here at home and then send them out to the Crimea was felt to be a process that would occupy much too long a space of time; but the moment the requisition for huts arose, we telegraphed to Lord Westmoreland at Vienna and to Lord Stratford at Constantinople, desiring them to send out instantly such huts as they could have constructed in those countries. Lord Westmoreland immediately forwarded all the huts he could procure by way of Trieste; and huts, and materials for constructing them, were also forwarded from Malta, and I hope we shall hear from Constantinople. If, therefore, any huts or buildings should be sent out by us from this country, as has been done, whenever they may arrive at the Crimea, they will, I hope, be rather accessories and additions to what have already been supplied than the furnishing an article not yet possessed by the army. (Cheers.) It is thus, then, that I answer the charge brought against us of having shown a heartless neglect and a gross indifference to the comfort and safety of what I believe to be the noblest army in the world. (Cheers.)

I have alluded to the manner in which our army is raised, and which I consider to be the best mode that any nation can adopt. What is the proof of that? Witness their conduct at the battle of the Alma. You have seen them both in attack and defence. I do not believe that any action was ever more difficult in point of attack than the carrying of the heights of Alma. Nor do I believe that you ever before heard an instance of such self-reliance, of such self-confidence, as was displayed at Balaklava, especially in sustaining the charge of the Russian cavalry by the 93rd Highlanders, under that tried soldier Sir Colin Campbell. (Cheers.) Every man remained in his place as they stood, two deep; as it has been well described, "as the Russians came within 600 yards, down went that line of steel, and before that fire and those immovable ranks the Russian horsemen turned and fled."

Well, what have you at Inkermann? The battle of Inkermann had been in preparation weeks before. It is said that so far back as the 24th of October a council of war was held by the Russians, and the whole of the battle was well arranged. The country, for upwards of a hundred miles round, was swept of everything. Every cart, every bullock, every horse, every carriage, was appropriated to bring troops to this action. I believe the course taken by the enemy was unexampled in the history of military warfare.

It was preconcerted that this attack should take place. Everything was to depend upon it; and the Emperor of Russia was assured that the result was certain. Our men keeping their lonely watch—after the battle came those after-memories which great events evoke—remembered that they heard the bells tolling in the churches of Sebastopol, and the murmur of great masses of men surging within the city. No doubt the religious ceremonies of the church were used to invest the occasion with a still more sacred character; no doubt appeals were made to the patriotism and religious feelings of those large masses of men. In the night heavy artillery was moved up to heights commanding our camp. As at Talavera, it was a surprise: men in the guise of deserters drew our sentinels from their posts, so that no alarm was given. At last came that terrible onslaught of 40,000 men on 8000. Yes. Well, the morning came, clouded by a heavy mist. There were 8000 men—as one right honourable gentleman has said, who brings a charge against the Government for that fact, as if the whole army consisted only of 8000 men. Those 8000 soldiers stood for hours beating back, with a fortitude and a courage more like gods than men, the attacking force that had come against them, and whose numbers were so great, that, as one body was repulsed, another and another came up and took its place. (Cheers.) I don't believe that, even going back to those battles which have acquired almost gigantic proportions from the length of time which has elapsed since they occurred, any instance can be adduced of such courage and unshaken bravery as those 8000 men displayed under circumstances so adverse and for so long a period against such immense odds. (Cheers.) That was a soldiers' battle. (Cheers.) There was, there could be, no manœuvring. There you saw the character of the English soldier—led, no doubt, by regimental officers, but it was the battle of the soldier standing in the ranks, and dying or conquering where he stood. (Cheers.) Well, who are these men who displayed such signal courage? I rejoice at the number of the letters that have been published in the newspapers written by soldiers. I rejoice that the people of England should know of what materials their armies are composed. The people of England are apt to look at a soldier as only fit for parade, and at the officer as exclusively possessing the moral and intellectual qualities of a soldier; but, after seeing the courage, the good conduct,

and the patience displayed by these men under unheard-of difficulties and sufferings, that opinion can no longer be entertained.

I ask the House to look at that army which is without a crime,
in which the office of judge-advocate is a sinecure, and mark the
simple piety shewn by the men writing to their wives, saying to
them that they are sure their children's prayers are heard, for that
God has mercifully protected them in the hour of battle. See the
touching words with which another speaks of the terrible loss of
the Coldstreams, and says " eight officers buried in one grave;
there was not a dry eye." How honourable are those words to the
officers who had inspired and to the men who felt such affection for
those gallant gentlemen who had died leading them to victory!
These were the men who showed mercy to the vanquished even
under a horrible provocation! But then comes the picture, too
truly drawn, I admit, by the right honourable baronet the member
for Droitwich, of the melancholy losses which our army have sustained. Among them is one, Sir G. Cathcart, who, to the
qualities of an accomplished soldier, added the enlightened views
of an able administrator. He had a combination of qualities of
the highest character, and his loss is a public loss, which will not
soon be repaired. (Cheers.)

It is impossible not to be struck, in reading the names of those
who have fallen, with the numbers of those who have gone to the
war from a sense of duty, and who have shown how little even
high position and those luxuries which wealth commands can
enervate the spirit of the English gentleman. (Cheers.) This
spirit has animated the army from the lowest to the highest
ranks. (Hear, hear.) I lament as much as the right honourable
gentleman can do the losses which we know that many even in
this House have sustained. (Hear.) I cannot look around me
without knowing that there are the parents and brothers and
other relatives of many of those gallant men who have so cheer-
fully laid down their young lives for the service of their country.
(Hear, hear.) But I turn from this painful subject, and say that
at any rate it is satisfactory to me to know that, great as this loss
has been—great especially in the high character of the men in
whatever rank who have fallen—yet in mere numbers that loss has
not been so large as on former occasions. England has undergone
greater losses at Talavera and Albuera, than it has sustained in
the Crimea. At Albuera, out of six or seven thousand men, only

eighteen hundred escaped unwounded, whereas in all the engagements in the Crimea, from the beginning to the end, there has not
been a greater loss by the sword in battle than 1350. More have
died—our whole loss amounts to no less than 4456 ; but this number
includes 2782 who have died of disease and of wounds, as well as
1350 who have been killed. Now, bad as that is, still it is much
less than what the exaggerated statements I have seen make our
losses to be. I have therefore tho ght it my duty to make that
statement in order to remove any more painful feeling than the
truth really warrants.

Let me say here, that we hope that the most public recognition
will be made which we can give, of the assistance we have received, and of the gallantry with which that assistance has been
given by our allies. It is a pleasure to read those private letters,
better evidence than any public despatches, of Lord Raglan, which
show the brotherhood that exists between the two commanders,
founded on the estimation which each has formed of the other
under trying circumstances. Our army cheered enthusiastically
the advance of General Bosquet's division when they came up at
that opportune moment and relieved the shattered battalions that
had been so long resisting the desperate attacks of the enemy ; and
they were right. Sir, I believe that this mixing together of the
armies of the two countries will effect a greater change in the
mutual relations between the two nations than can ever be achieved
by diplomatic notes and paper treaties. A French officer has
said that each army is acquiring the qualities of the other,—that
while we are acquiring the dash of the French, the French are
acquiring the firmness of the English. I believe in that union of
the two armies, which is the type of the union of the two nations,
we see the best prospect of attaining the great end we have in
view.

I ask those who, two months ago, were looking despondingly at
the state of things, to look at the position of England now ; and
to look at what has been the effect of the war already upon our
enemy. In previous wars we had alliances with countries who
took our money, but did not always fight, and the Governments
of which sometimes intrigued against us. We are now in alliance
with the most military and chivalrous nation in Europe, and we
see the opinion of Europe day by day coming nearer and nearer
to us, while Russia is placed in a state of isolation. A hostile

army is entrenched above her own chief arsenal, her fleet has been sunk by her own act, her forts along the coast of Circassia have been destroyed by her own hand. These are the effects of the first campaign. I ask, where can you find, in the history of England, a first campaign of not more than a few months' duration attended with such results? (Hear.) But still I hope to see more done, and for that purpose our army considerably increased; and if you, the House of Commons, think it ought to be, tell us so. (Hear, hear.) I tell you that the country is determined, at all hazard and at all cost, that the army of Lord Raglan shall be supported. (Loud cheers.) If the House of Commons does not answer to that feeling of the country, then the House of Commons must take the consequence (hear, hear), for, depend upon it, there is but one feeling upon this subject. We are engaged in a war which was entered upon with reluctance; we must carry it on vigorously to obtain that which is the object of all war—namely, peace; for peace to be obtained must be conquered. (Cheers.) Let no exertions be spared which will enable us by vigorous operations to gain that end. (Cheers.) I say further, if you think the Government worthy to be intrusted with those powers, then intrust them (hear); but I would sooner a thousand times turn out one government, or ten governments, than that any other policy should be adopted. (Hear, hear.) I care not in whose hands the conduct of the war is placed, provided it be carried on with vigour and determination; and provided the representatives of the people honestly and truly carry out the will of the nation, that the noblest of armies shall be assured of the means—so far as human means can avail—to obtain a perfect triumph. (Loud and long continued cheering.)

LONDON: PRINTED BY W. CLOWES AND SONS, STAMFORD STREET, AND CHARING CROSS.

THE CLOSE OF THE WAR,

OR THE

LOWEST TERMS OF PEACE.

SUBMITTED TO THE CONSIDERATION

OF

HER MAJESTY'S SECRETARY OF STATE FOR FOREIGN AFFAIRS.

BY

AN INCOME-TAX PAYER.

LONDON:

EDWARD STANFORD, 6, CHARING CROSS.

1854.

TO THE

RIGHT HON. THE EARL OF CLARENDON.

————————

My Lord,

Little apparently has yet been done by the
mighty armaments that have been sent forth from
the ports of England and France; few and insignificant are as yet the feats of English or French
arms to be recorded by the future historian of the
present struggle. The year is however wearing
apace, and events are progressing so rapidly, that
it is full time to consider and to be well advised
as to the terms on which the war is to be brought to
a close. It is not only possible, but it seems at
present in the highest degree probable, that no
battle will be fought between the Allied armies and
the Russians, that not a shot will be exchanged
between them on the Danube.

Nevertheless, it is time to consider the terms on
which peace, an honourable, and safe, and therefore
durable peace can be settled.

Twelve weeks ago, the Russians passed in great

A 2

force into the Dobrutscha—twelve weeks the most important to an army undertaking offensive operations across the Danube—during which time, with the Turkish forces only before them, defeat after defeat, repulse after repulse have been the unvarying result of their operations.

It now appears certain that all attempts to advance are abandoned as hopeless, and that the Russian generals must abandon their position, not only on the Danube, but in the Principalities, without waiting the issue of battle. With all the Turkish forces and the Allied armies before them on the Danube, and overwhelming Austrian numbers ready to pour into Moldavia, and to occupy the line of the Sereth and the Pruth, the most obvious military necessity would seem to dictate the withdrawal of the Russians from their present perilous position while it is yet time. It is not then premature to speculate on the Russians very speedily putting an end to the immediate cause of the war, by their compulsory and unconditional withdrawal from every portion of the Turkish territory on which they have set a hostile foot.

We shall have rescued from the grasp of the Autocrat the material pledge which he had seized, in order to coerce Turkey into submission to demands which have been pronounced by Europe to be wholly unfounded, and which never would have been made but for the conviction on the part of Russia that her strength was so great, and the decrepitude of

Turkey so far advanced, that the latter would have neither spirit nor power, under any provocation, to resent insult or to resent aggression, and that the other Powers would not be drawn as principals into a hopeless war in defence of a state which could do nothing to defend itself. The events of the last six months have shown that there was much probably of wilful falsehood, much probably of unconscious deception in the notions which prevailed, both as to the strength of Russia and the weakness of Turkey. Still it cannot be denied that Russia is, after making allowance for all exaggeration, a very great military power, and that Turkey, however it may defend itself on the Danube and the Balkan, could not single-handed have wrested the Provinces from Russia, or prevented the latter from establishing itself on the Dobrutschan shores of the Danube so as to dominate over the whole delta of that stream.

It is essential therefore that Turkey should be so strengthened, and that Russia should be so weakened as that for a long time to come the latter should feel itself obliged to forego its long cherished projects of aggression and aggrandizement—that it should be no longer tempted by the apparent easiness of the prey to renew its attacks.

Let us pause for a moment to recall the exact circumstances of danger in which the Western Powers felt it incumbent on them to give the Porte those counsels which they have since thought it due to themselves and to the world to support with the whole of their power. There was, as will be recollected, an attempt not less insidious in one sense than it was insolent in another, to obtain an extension and recognition of that protectorate over the Greek Church and people in Turkey of which Russia pretended to be *de facto* possessed.

It has often been shewn that there was nothing or at least very little in the mere terms of the existing treaties inconsistent with the integrity of the Ottoman Empire, or the independence of its Government; nothing calculated very seriously to wound the susceptibilities of Turkish pride. The danger and the wrong were in the use which an unscrupulous strong power like Russia could make of the concession by a weaker neighbour of any even the most insignificant right of interference in its domestic affairs.

The Russian Embassy at Constantinople claimed and established a power and an influence far beyond any thing expressed or intended by the Treaties. There was on the one side a continuous and increasing tone of aggression, the language, bearing and manner of insolent superiority; on the other hand a feeling of dependence and weakness; occasional struggles; hasty and ill advised ebullitions of discontent, followed by the habitual succumbing of the Porte to any threat which was very loud and very serious.

This was the state of things expressed by the

singular phrase " ab antiquo," in the Nesselrode
dispatches. It is a term not new in Russian
diplomacy when it has been found desirable to have
a quarrel with any weak State which has been
foolish enough to have treaty relations with the
Muscovite. The despatches of Count Nesselrode
were in this respect a very fair exposition of the
ideas of Russian statesmen—a very frank avowal of
Russian policy. In substance he said this : " The
Treaties are not enough for me, but under colour of
the Treaties the Russian Government has ' ab antiquo,' had an influence and exercised a control
which it claims to retain and will not part
with."

It was in fact the consciousness that this exclusive influence was from various causes slipping
away ; that Austria had about the Montenegro
affair used a style of diplomatic language which
Russia had deemed to be its peculiar privilege ; that
France had obtained a diplomatic triumph, however
paltry, in the wretched little affair of the Holy
Places ; and that the Divan was becoming more
and more in the habit of deferring to the counsels
of the English Ambassador. It was the knowledge
of these things, and the fear that the reforms made,
the concessions to the Rayahs, and the improved
organization of the military resources of the empire
might make the Turks inconveniently independent,
that led the Czar to believe that it was necessary to
strike the blow when he did. It was essential to

his policy to obtain something which should be a humiliation and a confession of weakness, something to shew to Moslem and Rayah, to Turk and Greek that the Divan had by a mere threat of his displeasure been driven back into trembling obedience, and that the Sultan reigned only through his contemptuous forbearance and moderation. It would have been a great *coup* if he had succeeded in spreading this opinion of Turkish weakness and Russian dictatorship throughout the East. In Europe the moral effect would have been scarcely less.

In this view the mere repulse of the Russians, is an advantage the importance of which it is scarcely possible to exaggerate. For a long series of years every war between Russia and Turkey has ended in some advantage, some acquisition of territory, some increase of power to the former, some serious diminution of power and of character to the latter. This gave to Russia a *prestige* of which she has made political capital. There was confidence on the one side. There was despondence on the other. The reversal of this; the mere fact that this last aggression has ended otherwise than all the former ones, will have produced a great and a permanent effect. The policy of Russia will have been unmasked and exposed. It will be scarcely possible for Russia to regain influence in the councils of the Porte. Its hostility is avowed; its designs are patent. The old feelings of enmity to the Muscovite will be embittered, and with the exasperation will be the consciousness that the contest is no longer hopeless. The Turk will have learned to rely on his own strength and on the support of the great Maritime Powers. He will have learnt also that Austria, the traditional enemy of the Ottoman power, is compelled by the necessity of her own position to become an ally, and is obliged for her own preservation to prevent any further growth of Russian power on the Danube.

It is important that the Turkish government should be well convinced, as it will be, of this.

But this is far from being enough. Something more is wanted to strengthen Turkey and to weaken Russia. This, however, must be something capable of commending itself to practical minds; something for the achievement of which it will be possible for the Western Powers to justify to their subjects and the world the continuance of the war after the evacuation of the Danubian provinces. The eyes of the world have been turned to the Baltic; and if the Baltic Powers had been fully alive to their duties in the war, much might have been done there which ought to be done. If the Baltic Powers had been fully impressed with the great truth that the struggle was one in which they were as much interested as Turkey; that it was not for the love of the Ottoman power or of Ottoman institutions or Turkish modes of government, that the Powers had taken up arms, but simply, honestly, and in perfect singleness of mind, to prevent the continued aggression of an overgrown power like Russia on any of its weaker neighbours. If the Baltic Powers had been ready to arm in support of a policy which they may any day themselves have to appeal to for protection; if, aware that the independence of the Baltic was as much at stake as the freedom of the Euxine, they had frankly and boldly taken their side in the contest, in all probability Finland would have been emancipated, and again annexed to the crown of Sweden. If Prussia had been animated by the spirit of a warrior or of a statesman, prompt to take advantage of a combination of circumstances that may never occur again, Poland might have been formed again into a kingdom; and the German and Lutheran provinces of Russia on the Baltic might have been rescued from the civil and religious tyranny of the Muscovite Tartar and of the idolatrous Greek Church. But these seem to be dreams. Sweden will not strike a blow for itself or for Finland. Prussia prefers to retain its dangerous neighbourhood to the Northern Bear. This being so, it is not for England and France chivalrously to prolong a contest for the purpose of giving back Finland to Sweden, or placing Prussia in that position of independence and strength for which it appears to have no desire. This being the condition of the Baltic Powers, apparently nothing can be done there beyond the blockade which has been established, and capturing and destroying the enemy's ships. The attention of statesmen must be now, therefore, as at the beginning of the contest, principally concentrated on European Turkey, the Danube, and the Black Sea.

Much is there within the power of the Allies, and easily to be effected.

In the first place all that was humiliating, all that was dangerous in the several Treaties between Russia and Turkey will disappear as of course. The latter will simply ignore and repudiate them. She will declare to her subjects and to the world, that she acknowledges no right of protection whatever in respect of any matter civil or ecclesiastical. While giving to her Christian subjects and to the friendly Powers the most satisfactory assurance that she will continue and enforce the laws already promulgated for securing perfect toleration and equal justice to all, she will declare that she acknowledges no right in any Foreign Power to interfere with her domestic policy, her legislation or government.

All right of protectorate in Russia over Servia, or over the Danubian Provinces, must remain absolutely abolished.

Notwithstanding some considerable elements of weakness in the position and political condition of the Turkish empire, it is impossible to look at the map of Turkey in Europe without seeing how exceedingly strong it naturally is for all purposes of defence. Constantinople is situated on a peninsula, capable of being easily protected by lines stronger and more defensible than the famous lines of Torres Vedras, with an advanced frontier at Adrianople not capable of being forced or turned except by an overwhelming military force supported by navies in command of both seas as was the case in 1829. The value of the line of Danubian fortresses, backed as this line is by the Balkans, has been well shewn by the sieges of Ibraila and Silistria in 1828 and 1829, and more recently and more vividly by the gallant and successful defences of Kalafat and Silistria in this war. Whatever may be the nominal strength of the Russian army, whatever may be the real strength of its military powers for offensive purposes, the events of the war in the years 1810, 1811 and 1812, those of 1828 and 1829, and of the present year, shew that Russia dare not advance without reducing the Danubian fortresses, and that the taking of them can only be effected by a vast expenditure of blood and money, and by a loss of time during which the Porte is able to gather, to concentrate, organize and discipline all the available forces of the Ottoman Empire. It is now known that even in 1829, if it had not been for the distraction in the counsels of the Divan, and for the treacherous inaction of some of the greatest Turkish leaders at the critical moment, Diebitsch and his army must have perished before Adrianople, notwithstanding the disasters on the Danube, the loss of Varna, and notwithstanding the fact that he was supported on both coasts by Russian fleets which rode absolute masters of the seas.

What should be done then is obvious. The Danubian line of defence must be restored to more than its strength before the disasters of the campaign of 1829. What was lost by the treaty of Adrianople must be recovered with good interest. On the Danube the fortress of Ibraila must be restored as a fortress of the first class, and again given up to the Turks, who, whatever may be the final destination of the Principalities, must have *têtes de pont* on the left side of the river opposite to all those fortresses of which they have shewn how well they can avail themselves. The line of Trajan's Wall should be restored and strengthened. The Government of the Sultan should be induced to take the necessary measures without delay to establish railway communication from Varna to Shumla, to be continued thence to Silistria and Rustchuk, which while opening the Bulgarian plains to commerce and civilization, will, with a well-organized flotilla of river steamers of war, render that line of defence impregnable by any force which it is probable that the Muscovites will be able to bring against it.

The Porte will doubtless be ready to avail itself of the engineering skill and military counsel

C

which are now at its disposal, not only to perfect this line, but to make the Bosphorus and the inland defence of Constantinople practically impregnable, that is to say, impregnable except against the regular approaches of an overwhelming force, with unlimited resources and abundance of time.

The most important question, but not one of any very great difficulty, will arise as to the ultimate destination of the Danubian Provinces. It is satisfactory to think that circumstances will have placed in the hands of enlightened and civilized Powers like England and France the futur. destinies of the hitherto hardly-used inhabitants of the Principalities. It has seemed strange that amidst all the deserved invectives against the unprincipled aggression of Russia, so little has been said or apparently even thought of the cruel wrongs inflicted without even a colour of provocation on the unoffending Wallachs. By treaties to which Russia was a party the practical independence of the Roumans was acknowledged, and they were placed under the special protectorate of the Czar. The result of that position has been that under pretence of a quarrel with the Porte, against whom they are protected by Russia, the protecting Power has exposed them to all the oppression, miseries and horrors of a military occupation by an army of Muscovites with its attendant hordes of Cossacks.

This too, as a matter of course, a thing done and to be done whenever a dispute arises between the two Governments—the Sovereign and the Protector.

It is the policy, as it is the duty, of the Western Powers, to make some compensation to that injured people for all the wrongs they have sustained. If one great result of the war be, as it may easily be, to provide for the future security and good government of the Principalities, humanity may well regard the prosperity and happiness of some millions of Wallachians and Moldavians as cheaply purchased by all the sacrifices of the Porte and its Allies. It is essential, however, not only that Turkey should lose nothing, but should appear to lose nothing by the war. The interference of the Frankish Giaour must leave nothing to rankle in the minds of the Ottomans—nothing for Russian intriguers to lay hold of hereafter to induce the belief that the Sultan has been as scurvily treated by his friends as he would have been by his enemies.

The preservation then of the present suzerainty of the Porte is essential : but preserving this, Moldavia and Wallachia should be united into one great feudatory principality, like Egypt or Servia, with a Prince receiving investiture from Constantinople, and owing certain military obligations for the defence of the Empire against attack.

With this merely feudal dependence and obligation, their actual internal independence and self-government should be effectually secured; and, pending the conclusion of the final arrangements for their regulation, it would not seem too much for the Allies to take themselves an active part in some Commission which might easily be devised to secure them a good internal organization, with institutions liberal and popular. All serfdom and all servile services of every kind would of course be abolished ; and an independent Judiciary established. With a few simple measures easily devised, with provisions for municipal government in the towns, and placed under some able and enlightened Prince, the Provinces would at once enter on a career of great and almost certain promise. Their neutrality and independence should form part of the policy of Europe, in the same manner as the neutrality and independence of Belgium and of Switzerland have hitherto done, and it should be declared by an European Congress that no invasion of their territory is to be permitted, and that any military occupation by any Power under any pretence, will be regarded and resented as a violation of the public law of Europe.

With respect to the lower part of the Danube something further may be, and ought to be done. Galatz should be made a free port and a free town, like Hamburgh or Frankfort-on-the-Maine, with its own government, open for commerce, and settlement to all the nations of the world, with perfect equality to all people and all creeds. There should be assigned to it a sufficient territory between the Sereth and the Pruth; and the whole of the delta of the Danube down to the sea: and it should be especially charged with the maintenance of the navigation of the Danube, the Sereth, and the Pruth. It should be made not only a free port, but an universal port in this sense, that every commercial nation in the world should be allowed to have its own factory and settlement there, as part of its own territory, subject to such regulations as should be desired for the good order and common safety of all. The whole world would be interested in the preservation and protection of such a port and territory; but it would, if necessary, be placed under the special joint protection of Turkey and Austria, as the two great Danubian States.

Under such circumstances and auspices the place would doubtless rapidly grow into the dimensions of a port worthy of its position on such a river. It would be impossible to calculate the effects of the impetus that would be given to the Danube and its great tributaries by such an arrangement, or of the civilizing influence which the commerce of such a port would carry into the heart of regions whose present state is the opprobrium alike of Mussulman and Christian Governments and Institutions. It would not be too much to expect that the wealth and enterprise of the citizens of another Amsterdam would make another Holland of the Danubian Delta.

Turkey rendered so far secure on her northern frontier, would be at liberty to proceed with those internal reforms and that military organization, which were the real and scarcely concealed causes of the present aggression of Russia. The experience of what has been already done by European science and discipline for the artillery and infantry, will doubtless induce the Sultan to proceed with ardour in the measures so far taken with such brilliant success, and to bestow equal care in the organization of the other branches of the service, the defects of which have been felt in the present war. It is not too much to expect, that in a few years Turkey will have a military force, in numbers, discipline and efficiency, worthy of its greatness as a state. The disaster of Sinope may possibly induce the Divan to proceed with no less vigour to give strength to its navy; and at the end of the war it would not be amiss if England and France were to sell to the Sultan, on easy terms and long credit, some of their most powerful screw ships of the line and frigates, and to leave a large portion of their crews there, so as to assist in the establishment and discipline of a powerful Black Sea fleet.

So much may be done for the strengthening of Turkey. Next for the weakening of Russia.

In the first place Russia must cease to be a Danubian power at all. The Danube is not a Russian river. It is not wanted by her for any commercial purpose; and the position which she has attained on the northern shores of the Danube has been so attained and has been used simply for purposes of aggression on Turkey, and for the obstruction of the navigation of the river. It may not be necessary absolutely to force her back to the Dneister, but she must not be permitted to retain Ismail. Above Ismail there will be seen on reference to the map, a territory now called Russian Moldavia, extending to the old line of Roman fortifications, along the Via Trajana. This must at all events be restored to Moldavia.

On the southern side of the Black Sea the remaining fortresses of Russia must be destroyed, and the absolute freedom of the whole line of coast from the Kuban to the Turkish frontier, and the independence of the whole of that mountain range, commonly called Circassia, must be insisted on and secured. The Transcaucasian provinces of Russia would seem to lie absolutely at the mercy of the Allies; and it is of the utmost importance that this opportunity should not be lost of wresting them entirely and finally from her grasp. It is not probable that the Russians have any hold on the affections of the native population, so that they would be disposed to fight on behalf of their present rulers. All communications by the Black Sea cut off, and Schamyl again in arms, backed probably by all the mountain tribes hitherto seduced by Russian gold and policy, the Transcaucasian army must be already in a very perilous position. The moment then that

all danger on the side of the Danube is removed,
what could be a more worthy reward for the distinguished commander of the Turkish forces, than that
he should be conveyed with a large army of his best
and most trusted troops, a considerable body of
picked soldiers of the Allies, and a foreign legion of
the active and stirring emigrants from Poland and
Hungary, who are panting for the work of war, to
take the command in Asia with ample powers and
means, and, gathering and organizing the Turkish
forces there, and acting in concert with Schamyl
and his Circassians, to pour a resistless torrent into
the Russian provinces, overwhelming the Russian
forces, and winning, like the Normans of old, a new
kingdom for himself and his followers. Such a
kingdom, extending from the Black Sea to the Caspian, and protected by the Caucasian range and the
invigorated spirit of the mountain tribes between it,
and by the military strength which such a sovereign
would know how to give it, might well maintain
itself against all the efforts of Russia; and being itself
open to the commerce of the world, would throw
open the Caspian and Central Asia to the same
beneficial and civilizing influence.

There remains the Crimea.—How often it occurs
in matters of high state policy, that the instinct of
the millions, which is in truth only another word for
practical common sense, points out to the hesitating
councils of statesmen, the course they should take.
And this instinct, the unmistakeable public opinion of

England and France, of all Europe, has declared that the military and naval reputation of the Allies will be stained—that the *prestige* of their power will suffer —and that of Russia preserved, perhaps increased, if, after such a struggle, Russia comes out of it. still retaining the Crimea and Sebastopol. She may have been blockaded—she may have been repulsed—she may have lost her position in and beyond the Circassian territory—but if she retains the Crimea, Sebastopol, and her fleet, she comes out of it practically unscathed, with little loss of reputation, and still less loss of real power. With the naval and military forces which the Western Powers have, or ought to have, at their disposal, the reduction of the Crimea is a mere matter of military mathematics.

It is impossible for Russia to concentrate, or if once concentrated, to maintain, in that remote peninsula, any thing like the numbers adequate to contend with the forces which the Allies, having the undisputed command of the Black Sea, could bring at any time, and with a few hours' steaming, from Varna, from Constantinople, from Trebizond, and if necessary from Circassia, to any of the harbours or creeks of the Crimea. The only real difficulty would be in the future destination of it. The Russian fleet would, of course, be either taken or destroyed, and it would probably be considered, under all circumstances, the safer policy also to destroy the whole of the fortifications of Sebasto-

pol. This done, it might be made into an independent state, under the safeguard and protection of
Turkey and the other powers of the Black Sea, who
would probably easily join in a league of mutual
defence against any Russian aggression. Turkey
would be at the head of a Black Sea confederation,
comprising the new kingdom of Georgia, the Circassian chiefs, and the Crimea. In addition to these
measures, the absolute power of the Porte to open
or close the Bosphorus to ships of war, should be
distinctly affirmed and maintained; and in exercise
of that right, the Porte should, by special convention with England, France, Austria, the United
States, and any other maritime state, having relations of commerce with the countries on the Black
Sea, permit a limited number of the ships of war to
be maintained in the Black Sea, and for that purpose to have ingress and egress by the Bosphorus
and the Dardanelles.

Such ought to be the terms of peace—such ought
to be the position of Russia at the close of the war.

It may be said, that Russia will never submit
to such terms—that she will retire within her shell
impenetrable, and wage a war of defence for ten, or
twenty, or thirty years, rather than submit to a
position so humiliating and so disadvantageous.

But what can she do? What can she hope to
gain by prolonging the struggle? She will be
found to lie as helpless as a harpooned whale, and
less capable of doing mischief. She will clearly be

unable to do anything on or beyond the Danube. What she has been unable to do against the Turks alone, will scarcely be within her power when the Danubian principalities are garrisoned by Austrian armies, supported by all the military and naval resources of England, France, and Turkey. To the Allies she can do no mischief; it is obvious that to them the continuance of the war will be a mere matter of a little extraordinary expenditure. After the first expense occasioned by the necessity of getting up in great haste the large armaments for the Baltic and the Black Sea, and transporting soldiers and horses and all the *impedimenta* of an army to the East, the war will not be a matter of any very heavy burthen to the Western Powers. Thirty or forty thousand soldiers may be maintained by England and France respectively when once the commissariat arrangements are perfected, pretty nearly as cheaply as they would at home; while the fleets at anchor, or cruising in the Black Sea, will not be much more expensive than in the chops of the Channel. And it is not to be overlooked, that so long as the English and French fleets and armies are employed together in the prosecution of a common object, the two countries need not be keeping up expensive armaments elsewhere to keep one another in check.

The commerce of England and France will proceed unaffected by the war; the raw materials hitherto supplied by Russia will come in abundance from other sources; and the new settlers will be also new buyers. To Russia, on the other hand, the continuance of the war is a continuance of a humiliation which such a Government can hardly venture to prolong the exhibition of to the people. The ships of war will be known to all the world as crouching behind batteries in the recesses of narrow channels. A rigid blockade will destroy all her foreign commerce, and all the revenue dependent on that commerce. The nobles and the people will be called on for sacrifices, will be subject to privations, without any thing to mitigate or compensate the infliction. To prolong such a state of things would imply absolute madness in the councils of the Czar, while every day would bring with it a fresh chance of fresh enemies. If the spectacle were prolonged of the humiliating position of Russia submitting, unresisting, to the pressure, and the insult of a blockade extending over her whole sea coast, it would not be in human nature long to resist the temptation. Sweden, Prussia, Persia would join in the chace, and plant themselves hungrily on the disabled prey.

Russia dare not long continue a war under such circumstances, with such impending perils; and painful and reluctant as the confession will be, she must confess herself overmatched, and sue for peace on such terms as the Powers may in their moderation be pleased to dictate. In such a case magnanimity is out of the question. The Powers have to take care that Russia is so weakened and Turkey so strengthened as to render the acquisition of any portion of Turkish territory hopeless, even in the eyes of the long waiting policy of the Cabinet of St. Petersburgh, and so to avert for very many years any fresh repetition of the aggression as improbable as it would be unlikely to succeed.

It may be suggested that Austria and Prussia will fall off, and be even hostile if the war be prolonged after the evacuation of the Principalities. That they will fall off is natural and to be expected, and their concurrence will be not wanted in the ulterior measures to be pursued. Prussia may be safely disregarded; and all that is required of Austria is to occupy the Principalities, and so interpose on that side a barrier between Russia and Turkey. To this she is bound by every obligation, and more effectually still by every consideration of what is due to her own honour and interest. It is not very probable that Austria will forego her own settled policy of preventing the growth of Russian power on the Danube in order to make war against the Allies in defence of the right of Russia to the Crimea, or Georgia, or Circassia, or for the purpose of keeping the Black Sea a Russian lake.

It may well be that Austria would be satisfied herself with the evacuation of the Principalities; but there is no Austrian or German interest to induce her to oppose the more vigorous measures which the English and French Governments may think it right to take in further prosecution of the common object, the permanent integrity of the Ottoman Empire and the independence of the Ottoman Government.

It is therefore morally certain that the Allies will meet with no real difficulties in proceeding in the course which their honour and interests require.

Such a peace as I have described is one within the power of France and England to conquer. It would protect Turkey probably for half a century, and throw back Russia in effectual aggressive power to what it was in Catherine's time. Such a peace would be a glorious termination of the war for France and England, worth many times over all the sacrifices which they will have been called on to make, and would probably lead to the repose of Europe for a period of peace as long as that which followed the fall of the military domination of the first Napoleon.

To England and France it is peculiarly essential that the war should have a termination thus happy and thus glorious. A common war prosecuted with generous emulation, with an entire absence on both sides of selfish projects of aggrandizement, with perfect good feeling and good faith, and ending in results which both may look back to with pride, will do much to cement the friendship which is the obvious interest of both, and to efface the bitter and painful recollections of past enmities.

If the war should on the contrary be permitted to

come to an unworthy and inglorious close, the self-love of each deeply wounded by the result, each would be tempted to accuse the timidity of the other's counsels, and new accusations of the worthlessness of French friendship and of the inveterate perfidy of Albion will probably arise, and give new life to the old feelings of national hatred which are happily dying out.

Have a care then, my Lord, not to be misled from the obvious course which is before you. The alliance between France and England is a great event, honourable to both—the war is a great and honourable war. Let the peace be no less great and no less honourable.

I am, my Lord,

Your Lordship's very obedient humble servant,

AN INCOME-TAX PAYER.